DEPRESSION AMERICA

DEPRESSION AMERICA

Volume 5

U.S. SOCIETY

GROLIER

EDUCATIONAL

About This book

The Great Depression is one of the most important periods of modern U.S. history. Images of breadlines and hungry families are as haunting today as they were at the time. Why did the crisis occur in the world's richest country, and how has it shaped the United States today? *Depression America* answers these questions and reveals a highly complex period in great detail. It describes the uplifting achievements of individuals, tells touching stories of community spirit, and illustrates a rich cultural life stretching from painting to movie-making.

Each of the six volumes covers a particular aspect of the period. The first traces the causes of the Depression through the preceding decades of U.S. history. The second examines the first term of Franklin D. Roosevelt and the New Deal he put in place to temper the effects of the crisis. The third volume studies how the Depression affected the lives of ordinary Americans. Volume 4 reveals the opposition FDR faced from both the political right and left, while Volume 5 explores the effect of the period on U.S. society and culture. The final volume places the Depression in the context of global extremism and the outbreak of World War II, the effects of which restored the United States to economic health.

Each book is split into chapters that explore their themes in depth. References within the text and in a See Also box at the end of each chapter point you to related articles elsewhere in the set, allowing you to further investigate topics of particular interest. There are also many special boxes throughout the set that highlight particular subjects in greater detail. They might provide a biography of an important person, examine the effect of a particular event, or give an eyewitness account of life in the Depression.

If you are not sure where to find a subject, look it up in the set index in each volume. The index covers all six books, so it will help you trace topics throughout the set. A glossary at the end of each book provides a brief explanation of important words and concepts, and a timeline gives a chronological account of key events of the period. The Further Reading list contains numerous books and useful web sites to allow you to do your own research.

Published 2001 by Grolier Educational
Sherman Turnpike
Danbury, Connecticut 06816

© 2001 Brown Partworks Limited

Set ISBN: 0-7172-5502-6
Volume ISBN: 0-7172-5507-7

Library of Congress Cataloging-in-Publication Data
Depression America
     p. cm.
    Includes indexes
    Contents: v. 1. Boom and bust – v. 2. Roosevelt's first term – v. 3. Countryside and city – v. 4. Political tensions – v. 5. U.S. society – v. 6. The war years and economic boom.
    ISBN 0-7172-5502-6 (set : alk. paper)
    1. United States–Economic conditions–1918-1945–Juvenile literature. 3. New Deal, 1933-1939–Juvenile literature. 4. Working class–United States–Juvenile literature. 5. United States–Social life and customs–1918-1945–Juvenile literature. [1. Depressions–1929. 2. New Deal, 1933-1939. 3. United States–History–1919-1933. 4. United States–History– 1933-1945. 5. United States–Economic conditions– 1918-1945.]

HC106.3 D44 2001
330.973'0916–dc21
                                              00-046641

For information address the publisher:
Grolier Educational, Sherman Turnpike,
Danbury, Connecticut 06816

Printed and bound in Singapore

For Brown Partworks
Volume consultant:
Dr. Heather Munro Prescott, Chair, Department of History, Central Connecticut State University
Managing editor: Tim Cooke
Editors: Claire Ellerton, Edward Horton, Christine Hatt, Lee Stacy
Designers: Sarah Williams, Lynne Ross
Picture research:
Becky Cox, Helen Simm, Daniela Marceddu
Indexer: Kay Ollerenshaw

CONTENTS

1

GOVERNMENT, INDUSTRY, AND ECONOMIC POLICY

*At the onset of the
Depression many
businesses supported
government moves
to deal with the crisis;
by the mid-1930s
they increasingly
opposed Roosevelt's
economic policies.*

The Great Depression was a
defining moment in the
relationship between gov-
ernment and business in the
United States. The Wall Street
Crash of 1929 and the inability of
many businesses to cope with the
onset of the Depression undermined the trust of many Americans in the country's business
leaders. Governments had long
supported the idea of a free-market
economy, which was subject to
economic factors like supply and
demand rather than government

*People gather outside an employ-
ment agency in 1934. The massive
slump in the economy following the
1929 stock-market crash resulted
in millions of job losses.*

Gross National Product

The following table shows U.S. Gross National Product (GNP), the total value of the goods and services produced by the economy, in billions of dollars. Economic activity reached its lowest point during the crisis of 1932 and 1933. It recovered steadily, apart from a dip in 1938, reflecting the economic crisis of the previous year. The increased production stimulated by the outbreak of World War II in Europe in 1939 finally brought the economy fully back to its pre-Depression strength.

	GNP $ billion
1929	103.8
1930	90.9
1931	75.9
1932	58.3
1933	55.8
1934	64.9
1935	72.2
1936	82.5
1937	90.2
1938	84.7
1939	90.4
1940	100.5

A farmer receives clothes from Red Cross volunteers in 1930. Hoover was initially reluctant to provide government aid for the needy, believing that individuals should help themselves.

regulation. However, that system proved incapable of coping with the worst economic depression the country had ever known.

There are two apparently conflicting interpretations of the relationship between government and industry during the Great Depression (see Volume 4, Chapter 1, "Left vs. Right"). For some people Hoover and, particularly, Roosevelt introduced a revolutionary degree of government intervention in the economy. For others the policies were not as radically innovative as this would suggest. One commentator on the New Deal said that its policies represented "only a change in the way of doing things. They were a means of working out new arrangements to bolster the existing order."

1. REGULATION VS. NONREGULATION

The truth lies somewhere between these two views. Although policies did increase government influence on firms, they did little to take away commercial and investment decisions from private businesses or to alter the nature of business in the country. Although federal involvement did grow, it drew on established traditions of government regulation.

In the 19th century federal involvement in business had often been promotional in nature, meaning that it was directed at encouraging private enterprises to undertake certain work that they might not otherwise wish to be involved in. Government aided the building of railroads, for example, by giving land grants and bounties to private companies, and used public ownership to build and run canals and roads.

After 1865, when industrial growth became more rapid, federal involvement became more regulatory in nature, trying to prevent business from acting in certain ways. One of the main thrusts of legislation was to limit the activities of trusts—huge corporations that tied together a number of concerns and shared many of the anticompetitive qualities of monopolies (see Volume 1, Chapter 1, "The United States, 1865–1914"). The legislation was not always effectively enforced,

Construction of the Boulder Dam, Boulder City, Nevada, 1934, one of many public works projects set up by the government to create jobs.

however. Successive administrations came to operate on the principle that trusts in themselves were not inherently undesirable, but that there were bad trusts.

2. HERBERT HOOVER

Throughout the 1920s Herbert Hoover's Republican predecessors followed a largely *laissez-faire* approach, which supported a free-market economy (see Volume 1, Chapter 3, "The Return to Normalcy," and Chapter 5, "The Fantasy World"). Hoover's popular reputation condemns him for doing nothing when the Great Depression broke out. Many historians, however, believe that Hoover intervened in the economy to an unprecedented degree after the crash of 1929. The fact that his efforts did not prevent the slide into depression reflected the scale and seriousness of the problem and the limited size of the federal budget in 1929: It accounted for only 3 percent of the Gross National Product (today, for comparison, it is more than 20 percent), a small amount that limited the effectiveness of any government spending.

Hoover believed that industrialists and businessmen were key to restoring confidence in the economy. In November and December 1929 he held a series of meetings with the country's heads of banks, railroads, industries, and utility companies. "A great res-

ponsibility and a great opportunity rest upon the business and economic organization of the country," he told them, stressing that government's intention was not to interfere in business: "It is a request from the government that you cooperate in prudent measures to solve a national problem." The key word was "cooperate." Hoover, and subsequently Roosevelt, preferred voluntary cooperation to direct government intervention.

SOCIAL ENGINEERING

Hoover summed up his beliefs on national prosperity as "a chicken for every pot and a car for every garage"; in other words, the nation's wealth should be shared. Such beliefs were reflected in his

Business Failures in the 1930s

The peak of business failures in the United States came relatively early in the 1930s. As weaker businesses went under, the failure rate slowed, and the total number of businesses returned to what it had been at the start of the decade.

	Total businesses (1,000s)	Total failures (1,000s)
1930	2,183	266
1931	2,125	282
1932	2,077	319
1933	1,961	196
1934	1,974	120
1935	1,983	122
1936	2,010	96
1937	2,057	94
1938	2,102	128
1939	2,116	147
1940	2,156	135

Government Intervention

Hoover's main type of indirect intervention came in the form of increasing cooperation between government and industry. He created committees and trade councils, and advocated cooperation between federal, state, and municipal authorities to create more public works projects to provide employment. He also maintained that the state should work with business and labor unions to solve problems instead of leaving them to solve disputes for themselves. There were limits to the action he would take, however. With his strong belief in individualism, he had little sympathy for farmers wanting handouts: "Take up religion" was his dismissive response.

"A chicken for every pot and a car for every garage…"

and many people condemned such agreements as a substitute for effective action.

ECONOMIC POLICY

One of the planks of Hoover's initial response to financial crisis was to keep interest rates low, making money available relatively cheaply to firms and individuals. The Federal Reserve added almost $300 million to available credit in the last weeks of 1929.

John Maynard Keynes, one of the outstanding economists of the century, praised Hoover's credit expansion as "thoroughly satisfactory." Such a policy was not supported by everyone, however. Andrew Mellon, secretary of the treasury since 1921 under Harding and Coolidge, advocated that Hoover should allow interest rates, like prices and employment, to find their own level. This was irresponsible, since a rise in interest rates would increase the already high rate of business failures in the economy and cause more job losses. For Mellon such failures were necessary to "purge the rottenness from the economy." He advised the president to "liquidate

consistent sympathy toward labor and working people. He urged employers not to cut wages, but to put employees on short-time working to create more jobs. Employers found it easier to agree in principle than to put such policies into practice, however,

In this cartoon by Rollin Kirby a cannon labeled "Roosevelt Administration" blasts a hole in a high wall labeled "Joe Grundy Tariff Wall." Grundy was a Pennsylvania businessman who supported the Smoot–Hawley Tariff Act of 1930 with such passion that it became known as the "Grundy Tariff." A flag labeled "Privilege" flying over the wall suggests that those who support high tariffs have the interests of the wealthy at heart.

labor, liquidate stocks, liquidate the farmers, and liquidate real estate." Hoover did not heed the recommendation.

Indirect Relief

The low interest rates injected money into the economy via the banking system. Meanwhile, public works programs such as the building of the Hoover Dam and San Francisco Bay Bridge put unemployed people to work.

Both cheap credit and public works were expensive for the government, whose coffers were

Rising Unemployment

During Hoover's last years unemployment rose. It had been 3.2 percent in 1929, an almost negligible amount, but by 1933 it had risen to 24.9 percent, a quarter of the working population. A year later it was 26.7 percent. It is estimated that during the worst period of unemployment, 34 million men, women, and children who would have contributed to business and industry were without work. These figures, of course, do not include the farm population. What this meant overall was that the people who really suffered were the people with no wages at all. Roosevelt did much more to alleviate the burden of unemployment through federal public works projects.

far from full. Credit encouraged some unsound businesses to get deeper into debt, a situation Mellon's *laissez-faire* approach would have avoided by letting them go under naturally. Hoover relaxed the bankruptcy laws and discouraged auctions of the assets of bankrupt firms, which were held by creditors to try to recoup some of their losses. This made it more difficult for banks to recover their debts, leading to increased bank failures and a loss of confidence in the system. Hoover injected more credit into the system, causing inflationary pressure.

The International World

Other pressure on the banking system came from overseas. In 1930 Hoover—against the advice of many economists—had pushed through the Smoot–Hawley Tariff Act. This act increased the already high import duties that theoretically protected U.S. business from foreign competition, in cases up to 50 percent. It helped spread the Depression to Europe, where countries found it hard to sell

An artwork by Reginald Marsh from around 1932 shows a vast crowd of unemployed Americans.

A man stands beside his Cadillac near the Lincoln Memorial, Washington, D.C. While millions of people struggled to eat, the rich continued to enjoy luxuries.

goods to America, a potentially huge market. World commodity prices continued to fall, which was particularly bad for American cotton and wheat farmers.

Europe had financial troubles of its own. On May 1, 1931, the Credit Anstalt, Austria's leading bank, collapsed. All German banks closed on July 13, and the British Labour government collapsed on August 24. On September 21 Britain abandoned the gold standard, the financial instrument that tied international currencies by linking the amount of money in circulation in an economy to the amount of gold a nation possessed.

With trade handicapped, European countries found it difficult to

Customers protest in the rain outside the Bank of the United States following its failure in 1931.

pay back their war debts to the United States. Hoover therefore placed a one-year moratorium on international debts, which made him unpopular at home, since the American public were determined to see their country's loans repaid. At the same time, confidence in

the dollar fell, and overseas savers began to remove gold from U.S. banks. Hoover was convinced that the country had to remain on the gold standard. Partly as a result, 5,096 banks with deposits of over $3 billion went bust in 1931 and 1932. By 1933 the U.S. banking system was at a virtual standstill.

FEDERAL DEBT

By 1931 Hoover's attempts to halt the Depression had run up a budget deficit of $2.2 billion. The next year credits of $2.3 billion were paid out, along with $1.6 billion in cash. By the end of Hoover's presidency in early 1933 the federal government was spending $500 million a year more than it had in 1928.

Hoover's endeavors did not halt the Depression, for which he carried—and still carries—an unfair amount of blame. What they did do was begin a process that Roosevelt would continue, and for which Hoover received an unfairly small degree of credit. In 1934 Rexford Tugwell, one of

Roosevelt's celebrated Brain Trust, said, "We didn't admit it at the time, but practically the whole 'New Deal' was extrapolated from programs Hoover started."

Hoover continued to push business into lowering dividends, cutting profits, and reducing the cost of living while allowing wages to remain high. The United States had the highest real wages in the world during the period. His attacks on those he called the "bitter-end liquidationists" also stymied the business and financial community, who became

Jesse Jones (second from right), chairman of the Reconstruction Finance Corporation, at a hearing of the Senate banking and currency committee, February 1936.

convinced he was prolabor and antibusiness. In some respects they were right. Hoover regarded the stock exchange as parasitic and destabilizing, and insisted on federal investigation of its practices, a move that iself caused a fall in the value of stocks.

U-TURN

Running up budget deficits, Hoover became increasingly convinced, to the point of obsession, of "the absolute necessity of a balanced budget," which he believed to be "the foundation of all public and private financial stability." In a switch that belied his lack of confidence in how to control the Depression, he proposed cutting public spending and raising taxes. He denounced any

public spending and called for an increase in taxes.

Critics pointed out that cutting public spending and raising taxes would reduce spending power even

•

"…the absolute necessity of a balanced budget…"

•

more, but Hoover was deaf to this objection. He cut spending and turned his back on one of the foundations of his initial anti-Depression program—the need for ambitious public works.

False Confidence

Despite Hoover's attempts to convince the public that economic recovery was imminent, businesses continued to fold, and production figures slid downward. The index of industrial production fell from 114 points in August 1929 to 54 points in March 1933. Business construction, which had totaled $8.7 billion in 1929, fell to $1.4 billion in 1933. There was a 77 percent decline in manufacturing in the same period.

THE DEMISE OF INDIVIDUALIST BUSINESS

It was easy to blame the excesses of the stock market and business for the crisis, but business itself was not to blame. The problem was, rather, the lack of regulation in business. Business practices including speculation and overproduction had contributed to the causes of the Depression. To recover from it and prevent another occurring, it became apparent, business now faced a stark choice: regulate itself or be regulated. The old emphasis on individualism was fine up to a point, but not when businesses were allowed to act against the needs of society or the state.

The new emphasis, therefore, had to be on corporate efforts and corporation philosophy. Business had to be planned in such a way as to prevent the capitalist economy

Treasury Secretary Andrew Mellon is depicted atop a mountain labeled "Aluminum Monopoly" in this cartoon from April 1937. Mellon's Aluminum Company of America had virtually cornered the world market in the raw materials needed to make aluminum. In 1937 the government charged it with monopolizing aluminum manufacturing, and it was ordered to break up its holdings.

from overheating. Henry Harriman, head of the New England Power Company, said: "We have left the period of extreme individualism. Business, property, and employment will be best maintained by an intelligent, planned business structure."

BANK REFORMS

In 1931 the president called bank bosses together and asked them to pool their resources to create a credit reserve for the less healthy banks. He was surprised and angry when they told him that

Favoritism in RFC Loans

When Roosevelt signed the bill to create the Reconstruction Finance Corporation (RFC), he stressed that it was there to help the little guy. However, when the RFC reported its loans to Congress, a different picture emerged. In April 1932 Hoover had boasted that $126 million in RFC loans had gone to banks in 45 states. In fact, more than half this sum had been granted to just three large banks. This led to criticism of the RFC for favoritism in granting loans.

In June Charles G. Dawes, president of the RFC, resigned, stating that he had to return to Chicago to take charge of the Central Republic Bank. A few weeks later the RFC granted the same bank $90 million—and this at a time when its own reserves were just $95 million. Ironically, the loan did not save the bank. It had to undergo extensive reorganization and then, after litigation, repay the loan.

Later on, Atlee Pomerene, Dawes' successor, authorized a loan to the Cleveland Bank, of which he was a director, in the amount of $12 million. When this was disclosed, the whole system seemed to smell of corruption. How, critics asked, could the unemployed be denied federal aid when huge amounts of money were being siphoned off into the coffers of large banks? There was no easy answer; but when the RFC began to operate with less secrecy, loans to big banks reduced considerably.

they felt it was the government's responsibility to support the weaker banks. The bankers later set up a National Credit Association, but it came to virtually nothing and was soon abandoned.

THE RECONSTRUCTION FINANCE CORPORATION

Eugene Mayer, governor of the Federal Reserve Board (FRB), came up with an alternative that involved making loans to banks, railroads, and insurance companies using taxpayers' money. Hoover reluctantly accepted the idea, believing that it might develop confidence in the system. In so doing, he at last fully embraced direct government action.

More than two million employers displayed the Blue Eagle symbol of the National Recovery Administration to show that they were part of the scheme.

When the Reconstruction Finance Corporation (RFC) came into being in January 1932, banks were failing and gold was flowing out of the country as investors sold off their securities in exchange for the metal. Worse still, the Federal Reserve member banks had watched their reserves drop to within $50 million of the amount the law insisted they must hold. During its first year the RFC managed to distribute only $1.5 billion of the $2 billion at its disposal, most of which went to banks and trust companies.

Bank Debts Increase

Banks could only accept RFC money as loans—the RFC could not buy stock—which in the long term only added to their debts. This did little to help ensure their stability: What the banks needed was more capital, not more debt. The result, as one contemporary observer put it, was that the RFC gradually bankrupted banks in its efforts to save them. For five months details of the work of the RFC were kept secret because it was feared that knowledge of it might provoke a loss of confidence and a run on the banks.

HOOVER AND BUSINESSMEN

Hoover's attitude to business was ambiguous. Privately he complained that businessmen were greedy liars, but they belonged to the America he had always known,

and as part of this system, he considered them relatively safe.

Hoover's real anger was reserved for those who wanted to change the system or who favored greater powers for the federal government. Such critics included president-elect Franklin D. Roosevelt. This difference in opinion was an important factor in the almost total lack of cooperation between the two in the months from the November election to Roosevelt's inauguration in March 1933 (see Volume 2, Chapter 1, "The Election of 1932").

3. ROOSEVELT AND ECONOMIC POLICY

When Roosevelt took office, the nation was in a severe state of depression. Business failures and unemployment were high, while production and sales were low. The new president's primary task, therefore, was to address the economic crisis and implement measures to pull America out of its slump and to devise policies and reforms to prevent such a situation from happening again (see Volume 2, Chapter 2, "The First Hundred Days").

FEDERAL REGULATION

While federal regulation was already well-established by the time of Roosevelt's inauguration, it increased significantly during his administration.

In the short-term Roosevelt recommended the setting up of regulatory agencies in addition to the RFC. They included the National Recovery Administration (NRA), the Agricultural Adjustment Administration (AAA), and the National Labor Relations Board (NRLB), all of which were to have a limited life (see Volume 3, Chapter 2, "Shadow over the Countryside," and Volume 4,

Emperor Jones and Cactus Jack

One of the most important figures in Roosevelt's New Deal team was banker Jesse H. Jones (1874–1956), who presided over the government's credit arrangements. Jones came from a tobacco-farming family in Texas but went into business in Houston. By 1910 he was Houston's leading businessman. In 1928 Jones, a committed Democrat, brought the Democratic National Convention to the city.

In 1932, when Herbert Hoover established the Reconstruction Finance Corporation to hand out low-interest loans to banks, credit unions, and other financial institutions, he was eager to have both Republicans and Democrats on its board and offered one of the positions to Jones, who accepted. Jones believed that the RFC concentrated too much on eastern banks, and he tried to push it to extend its credit more widely.

When FDR became president, he asked Jones to become chairman of the RFC. To increase bank loans to business, Roosevelt also allowed the RFC to buy stocks in banks, rather than make loans to them that they might be nervous about repaying. Although the RFC bought $1.3 billion in bank stock, bank loans continued to decline from $38 billion in 1930 to $20 billion in 1935. As the importance of the RFC—and of Jesse Jones—grew to combat the continuing problems, the agency became the funding source for federal agencies such as the Federal Emergency Relief Administration, the Farm Credit Association, and the Resettlement Administration.

In 1939 the Federal Loan Agency was created to control the RFC and other agencies. Jones became its administrator and also became secretary of commerce in the cabinet. One senator remarked, "I do not think with the exception of the president of the United States any man in the United States ever enjoyed so much power." By 1940 the RFC had loaned over $8 billion to businesses and financial institutions.

Jones was closely associated with vice president and fellow Texan banker John Garner. The colorful pair became known as "Emperor Jones" or "Uncle Jesse" and "Cactus Jack."

Jesse Jones, photographed around 1940, led the RFC during its period as the United States' "superbank," providing loans and buying stock in a whole range of financial institutions.

The Federal Reserve System

The Federal Reserve System (Fed) was created in 1913 to act as the central bank of the United States, a role it still performs today. Its chief responsibility is to oversee the U.S. money supply to prevent, for example, periods of high demand that leave banks unable to pay out their deposits; it does this by issuing coins and currency and by regulating the amounts that member banks can lend. It also sets the discount rate at which it lends money to banks. The Fed operates as a second level of regulation for commercial banks. Since 1863 banks had been chartered either at state or national level; the creation of the Fed added an additional level of control, with a system of examiners to check on the affairs of member banks.

The Fed was created relatively late; Britain's central bank, the Bank of England, for example, had been created in the 1690s. One reason was that states feared centralized control of the system. Partly for that reason, when the Fed was set up, it comprised a system of 12 closely interlinked Federal Reserve Banks throughout the country, brought together by a central board of governors. The most important was, and still is, in New York.

Modern economists agree that the Fed did not prevent the collapse of the bank system at the start of the Great Depression. Part of that reason was that in 1930 two-thirds of U.S. banks were not part of the Federal Reserve System; it also failed, however, to prevent the collapse of member banks like the Bank of the United States. Some economists go further and blame the Fed not only for helping start the Depression but also for prolonging it.

These critics point out that the Fed continued to tighten its monetary policy in 1928 and 1929, at a time when the U.S. economy needed increased money supply to stimulate demand, contributing to the massive bank failures. Again in the mid-1930s, they argue, the Fed's tight control of monetary policy contributed to the recession of 1937, when unemployment figures started to rise again.

Chapter 6, "The Unionization of Labor").

In the longer term FDR introduced many more measures that extended the scope of federal regulation. Among the acts he

Cartoon showing General Hugh Johnson flying a kite labeled "NRA," while runners bombard it with "Criticism." Lute Pease (1869–1963), the cartoonist, was commenting on the controversial nature of the National Recovery Administration.

issued were the Securities Act (1933) and Securities and Exchange Act (1934), the Banking Acts of 1933 and 1935, and the Holding Company Act (1935). In addition, the Federal Communications Commission extended government regulation to the broadcasting industry, which had been growing in importance since the 1920s; the transportation system also became subject to federal controls. The Robinson–Patman Act (1937) extended federal control over business practices. Although critics of extended federal regulation argued that such a policy smacked of totalitarianism, Roosevelt was adamant that he supported American democracy. He protested that his aim was to clean up the dubious practices

Workers during a labor strike at the Ford Motor Company, 1937. Roosevelt was sympathetic toward workers and labor unions, and union membership increased from three million in 1933 to nine million in 1939.

of private business and, in so doing, to rekindle confidence in the economy as a whole.

BANKING REFORMS

When Roosevelt took office, the banks were in a mess. The huge number of bank closures during Hoover's presidency were largely a result of the vast number of banks in operation and the lack of structure in the banking system. Most banks were single operations, few banks had branches, and the Federal Reserve, the central bank established to support the system, was inadequate for its task.

As a first reform measure, Roosevelt declared a four-day "banker's holiday." When it was over the banks were allowed to reopen only under presidential powers to safeguard both shareholders and depositors.

FDR on NIRA

The National Recovery Administration (NRA) was set up to oversee public spending and industry self-regulation. However, in 1935 the Supreme Court ruled it unconstitutional. Roosevelt's argument for the NRA ran as follows:

"The change from starvation wages and starvation employment to living wages and sustained employment can, in part, be made by an industrial covenant to which all employers shall subscribe. It is…in their interest to do this because decent living widely spread among our 125 million people eventually means the opening up…of the richest market the world has known. It is the only way to utilize the…excess capacity of our industrial plants….

"The idea is for employers to hire more men…by reducing the work hours of each man's week and at the same time paying a living wage for the shorter week. No employer and no group of less than all employers in a single trade could do this alone…. But if all employers…agree to act together and at once, none will be hurt and millions of workers, so long deprived of the right to earn their bread in the sweat of their labor, can raise their heads again. The challenge…is whether we can sink selfish interest and present a solid front against a common peril."

Banking Acts

Under an Emergency Banking Act about 5 percent of banks—around 1,000—were liquidated, while the rest were given a certificate of soundness. In turn the government's RFC bought stock in the banks and so became a major shareholder. In effect, some thought, the center of American banking had been shifted from Wall Street to Washington.

Roosevelt's banking reforms were characteristically conservative. He opted not to nationalize the banks but to reform the existing system with government support.

Among other provisions the Banking Act of 1933 created the Federal Deposit Insurance Corporation to insure bank deposits. The insurance feature was designed to restore depositors' confidence in the banks and so avert panic runs on the banks, and thus reduce bank collapses.

The Banking Act of 1935 gave the Fed greater powers and made central banking integral to American banking. Again, Roosevelt was conservative in his approach, prefering to modify the existing Federal Reserve set-up rather than push for government ownership of all the banks.

Monetary Policy

Among the ways governments can influence the economy are monetary policy—the control of the amount of money in circulation by altering interest rates and other measures—and fiscal policy, which relates to a government's taxing and spending. The main thrust of Roosevelt's monetary policy in 1933 was economic expansion. He believed that monetary expansion would achieve price inflation, which would encourage the demand for goods and services. This expansion was achieved indirectly through banking reforms, which gave depositors the confidence to invest their money with the banks, thereby increasing bank deposits and, as a result, putting the banks in a favorable position to make loans, thus augmenting the country's money supply.

Gold Policy

Then in November 1933 FDR announced a new gold policy, designed to reduce the dollar's gold content. Daily throughout January he authorized purchases of gold that kept the U.S. price of gold higher than prices abroad. As a consequence gold production in and gold imports into the United States rocketed. Individuals and businesses exchanged their gold for U.S. dollars at a high price, then deposited their dollars in U.S. banks, thus increasing total

Automobile industry tycoon Henry Ford (1863–1947) was one of the employers who ignored the codes of the NRA.

A closed bank at Haverhill, Iowa, September 1939. Even by the end of the decade the economy was still not in great shape. It would take World War II to truly restore the U.S. economy.

deposits in U.S. banks and the total amounts banks could loan.

The flow of gold into America resulted in monetary expansion at a rate of 11 percent per year from 1933 to 1937; the expansion played an important part in economic recovery in the period. By mid-1937, concerned that the rate of expansion was too rapid, Roosevelt let the FRB offset the flow of gold into the country. However, the measures the FRB took contributed to a new recession in 1937 and 1938.

FISCAL POLICY

Fiscal policy during Roosevelt's presidency was largely ineffective. Like Hoover, he started by trying to balance the budget, believing that it would restore people's confidence and so encourage

them to invest. Balancing the budget was not easy at a time of economic depression, however. It was made harder by the need to finance costly New Deal programs, which necessitated raising taxes. However, raising taxes too steeply would have depressed the economy still further, so Roosevelt compromised on balancing the budget by allowing some deficit

spending. Federal deficits almost doubled from $2.6 billion in 1933 to $4.4 billion in 1936.

Economists such as John Maynard Keynes later proposed that in a depression it was preferable to stimulate recovery by deficit spending rather than balancing the budget. At the time, however, even New Dealers did not welcome deficits and strove to keep them low. It was only near the end of the 1937–1938 recession that FDR wholeheartedly embraced deficit spending.

Taxation

The chief aims of Roosevelt's taxation policy were to raise revenues for new programs and to redistribute income and wealth, while at the same time balancing the budget. His chief tax targets were rich people and businesses. Some of the most important reforms he recommended came in 1935: a graduated tax on corporations to monitor the growth of monopoly, a tax on dividends received by holding companies, an increase in the maximum income tax rate on individuals from 63 percent to

The U.S. Chamber of Commerce

Set up in 1912 to promote and protect business interests, the U.S. Chamber of Commerce was a conservative organization that opposed many of Roosevelt's New Deal policies. Although it initially offered to cooperate with the administration, in September 1934 the chamber's director informed the president of "a general state of apprehension among businessmen of the country" regarding the government's failure to balance the budget and the growing intervention of government in private business matters. Roosevelt dismissed the chamber's statement and urged chamber officials "to cooperate for recovery." The Chamber, however, refused to toe the party line and retaliated by opposing many of the New Deal acts, including the NRA and AAA. The Chamber's magazine, *Nation's Business*, continued to campaign for greater freedom for businesses.

Rex Tugwell inspecting allotments at Berwyn, Maryland, November 1935. Tugwell was a member of Roosevelt's Brain Trust.

79 percent, and an inheritance tax. The following year Roosevelt asked Congress to pass a tax on profits businesses did not share out among their shareholders.

All these reforms were intended to spread wealth and income more evenly. In reality they had little effect on the distribution of wealth and made the business world, which suffered worst from their effects, increasingly hostile toward the president.

REFORMING INDUSTRY

The New Deal's early emphasis on working with business rather than attacking monopolies and trusts reflected the priority the American public placed on getting business back on a level footing so

that it could provide work for the unemployed. The New Deal thus began with the provisions of the National Recovery Administration (NRA).

The NRA amounted to a system of codes underwritten by the government and designed to solve problems of employment practice. It attempted to negotiate fair prices, wages, and working hours with employers and labor representatives in all the major industrial sectors. These codes of fair practice, however, were in fact drawn up mostly by representatives of big business, which annoyed both small businessmen and organized labor alike. Ultimately, the NRA did little to bring about industrial recovery. This contributed to its final demise in 1935, when the Supreme Court ruled it unconstitutional (see Volume 4, Chapter 2, "The Supreme Court").

ADDITIONAL ACTS

In the mid-thirties FDR pushed through government several acts that were specifically designed to help industry. The Loans to Industry Act of 1934, in retrospect, seems to be simply an extension of the lending activity of Hoover's RFC. The Securities and Banking Act and Securities and Exchange Act (1934) were set up to regulate practices on the stock exchanges as a result of the unethical activities on the New York Stock Exchange in the 1920s. Both were reminiscent of ideas originally introduced by Hoover. Even the National Labor Relations Act (1935), or Wagner Act, was no more than an extension of the Norris-La Guardia Act of 1932, which made it illegal to enforce so-called "yellow dog" contracts that forbade employees from joining a labor union.

BIG BUSINESS

Roosevelt's reformist Democratic predecessors had often targeted big business, particularly in the form of trusts or monopolies. Many, however, had come to accept that there were certain economic arguments in favor of consolidation of industry in large corporations. In his book *American Capitalism* economist J. K. Galbraith took the view that business consolidation created a sound base for strong buying and also for strong selling. This idea was built on the ability of large concerns to save money by what are called economies of scale.

New Dealer David Lilienthal (1899–1981), who worked on the board of the Tennessee Valley Authority and was later its

---

Sewer Workers in Suits

Despite government attempts to rationalize business, not all businessmen avoided the worst aspects of the Depression. When Harry Hopkins, director of the New Deal relief program, took leading businessman Frank Walker on a tour to inspect the workings of the program in his home state of Montana, Walker came across a shocking sight. Former businessmen were laying sewer pipes dressed in their business suits because they had no money to buy overalls. One of them said of the situation before he got the work, "I stood in front of the bake-shop down the street and wondered just how long it would be before I got desperate enough to pick up a rock and heave it through that window and grab some bread to take home."

---

chairman, was eager to stress the importance of big business in investing in technological development. This underlined the early New Deal approach to business consolidation and trusts. They were a necessary evil that could, in the end, benefit society and the consumer.

BUSINESS AND THE NRA

After the demise of the NRA much of Roosevelt's sympathy for big business evaporated. During the NRA period he found corporate leaders and businessmen highly unsatisfactory partners. Many, including carmaker and right-wing sympathizer Henry Ford, flouted the provisions of the NRA, often openly. Others quietly skirted around those provisions to which they objected.

ANTI-BIG BUSINESS FEELING

Another incident that turned the president against freedom for big business was the sudden emergence of Louisiana senator Huey Long (see Volume 4, Chapter 3, "Huey Long"). Long hated

Former governor of Louisiana, Huey Long (1893–1935), talking to newsmen in 1935. Long believed the government should tax wealthy industries and big businesses heavily to provide for the poor.

The Brain Trust blamed price-fixing by corporations. They lobbied the president to start a new trust-busting campaign, but FDR was not prepared to move quickly.

The main cause of the recession was bad policy. In the fall of 1937, after four years of rapid recovery, the government let the Fed restrict monetary expansion (see box, page 16). At the same time, it made renewed attempts to balance the budget to avoid having to finance costly deficits.

With four million more people out of work by March 1938 FDR launched a massive spending and lending program. Three months later the country was back on the road to recovery.

THE TEMPORARY NATIONAL ECONOMIC COMMITTEE
Set up in June 1938 after the 1937 recession, the Temporary National Economic Committee was charged with studying America's ongoing economic problems. By the time the 12-member committee had been selected, its brief had expanded to

what he called the business "moguls" and threatened to deal with them if he got to the White House. The popularity of Long's message and his Share-Our-Wealth campaign made Roosevelt aware of just how much anti-big business feeling there was. In 1936 his State of the Union Address confirmed his more truculent anti-big business stand (see Volume 2, Chapter 6, "The Election of 1936"). He condemned the "entrenched greed" and "selfish power" of the men who ran the country's great corporations. They had proved themselves untrustworthy and selfish. They had, therefore, he argued, left themselves open to more federal constraint.

NEW RECESSION
In 1937, at the peak of economic recovery, a new recession occurred. Industrial production fell by 33 percent, national income by 13 percent, wages by 35 percent. Unemployment started to rise again.

FDR, his aide Tommy Corcoran, and vice-presidential running mate Henry Wallace cover their ears as a gun labeled "No Third Term" explodes above them. The cartoon suggests that FDR ignored popular disapproval of his run for a third term in 1940.

National Economic Planning

Roosevelt's assembly of advisers, the Brain Trust, was committed to the formation of large economic units, with the government playing an important role in running the country's economy. This put national economic planning high on the agenda. The main question was whether there should be any compulsion in the government's approach. Even businessmen, used to almost complete freedom to do as they pleased, welcomed government initiatives that might prevent them from going bankrupt. Indeed, virtually all economic groups, from farmers to financiers and economic leaders, recognized the need to reform ideas on government intervention. Two members of the Brian Trust in particular, Hugh Johnson and Rexford Tugwell, influenced economic planning. Both agreed on the need for government economic intervention; but while Johnson advocated planning by partial cooperation, Tugwell insisted on planning by overall compulsion.

include a thorough investigation of the economic system.

Three sets of responses emerged from the committee's studies. One group accepted that for large sectors of the economy, trusts and monopolies were inevitable and even desirable, and favored government regulation of industry. The second group felt that economic recovery was inhibited by the monopolistic fixing of prices and wages, and supported government action to break up trusts and monopolies, thereby removing the need for further government regulation. The third group concluded that the way forward for government was through taxing and spending, without the need for federal regulation. This last response reflected an argument put forward in J. M. Keynes's *General Theory of Employment, Interest, and Money* (1936) in favor of permanent deficit spending by the government in order to encourage public spending and maintain healthy employment levels.

ECONOMIC RECOVERY

Ordinary Americans in the late 1930s were feeling less in control of their lives. Bigger companies, more cars, and a less personal atmosphere left many feeling they were little different from the machines they were producing. This was exacerbated by a feeling of insecurity brought on by the Depression and the government's inability to end it. More and more people depended for a job on industry and business, big or small. Still, most Americans clung to the ideal that the spirit of the pioneer and the entrepreneur would see them through. It would take a world conflict to see America turn the corner and head back to commercial recovery.

Hoover vs. FDR

One of the lasting debates about the Great Depression concerns the effectiveness of the approaches taken to the crisis by Herbert Hoover and Franklin D. Roosevelt. Although each man criticized the other at the time, their responses in fact showed certain similarities. Both faced the same challenge: How to deal with the biggest economic crisis in U.S. history. And both faced the same set of political parameters. The belief that the budget must be balanced was a given in U.S. politics, as was a deep-seated suspicion of federal intervention at the expense of states' rights. In addition, their scope for direct intervention was limited by the relatively small size of the federal government at the start of the 1930s.

Both Hoover and Roosevelt began by working within these limits in their efforts to improve economic conditions in the United States. Both preferred to urge business leaders to cooperate and communicate with government and labor organizations, setting up committees and agencies to bring all sides together. A direct line connects Hoover's early discussions with business leaders to Roosevelt's introduction of voluntary codes under the National Recovery Administration. It was only after the election of 1936 and the recession of 1937 that Roosevelt became more radical in his assault on big business, preferring regulation rather than cooperation.

In terms of monetary policy, too, there was considerable continuity between the two administrations. Both men believed that the banking system should be stabilized, but neither wished to nationalize the banking industry or establish a new central bank to replace the decentralized Federal Reserve System. Economists argue that the recession of 1937, like the onset of the Great Depression itself under Hoover, was made worse by the Fed's tight monetary control.

Roosevelt's initial fiscal policy was, like Hoover's, committed to balancing the budget, a standard of U.S. economic thought. The New Dealers were careful to pay for federal programs by tax increases and other measures. It was only when faced with rising relief rolls again in 1937 that Roosevelt accepted that he had little choice but deficit spending, running the national account into debt in order to try to kick-start economic activity.

—— SEE ALSO ——

◆ Volume 1, Chapter 1, The United States, 1865–1914

◆ Volume 1, Chapter 3, The Return to Normalcy

◆ Volume 1, Chapter 5, The Fantasy World

◆ Volume 2, Chapter 6, The Election of 1936

◆ Volume 4, Chapter 2, The Supreme Court

◆ Volume 4, Chapter 3, Huey Long

◆ Volume 4, Chapter 4, The Right-Wing Backlash

EQUALITY FOR SOME

In the depths of the Depression the United States looked after its own at the expense of so-called "outsiders." Many of these blacks, Native Americans, and Hispanics were American citizens, however. They suffered discrimination, lack of financial opportunity, deportation, and even lynching. Overall, however, the thirties did bring some improvement for America's ethnic populations.

In the early years of the Depression it was the most vulnerable segments of American society who suffered the greatest humiliations. Prominent among those who felt few of the initial benefits of the New Deal were African Americans, Native American Indians, Mexican migrant farm workers, and many of the poor immigrants who filled the sweatshops of the large cities. The treatment of the "hyphenated Americans" echoed earlier trends in U.S. society. During the 1890s financial crisis had revived "nativist" protests against "un-American" newcomers to the

A drinking fountain for blacks in a streetcar terminal in Oklahoma City, 1939. Segregation was a fact of daily life throughout the South.

country; in the 1920s isolationist policies led to the effective ending of mass immigration. These "outsiders" were usually the first to

Uneven Distribution of Relief

One black American wrote Roosevelt to protest the unfair distribution of relief supplies in the South. The eloquence of his case shines through the letter's lack of formal spelling or grammar and is an indictment of the attitudes of white Americans.

"Dear Mr. President
"Would you please direct the people in charge of the releaf work in Georgia to issue the provisions + other supplies to our suffering colored people. I am sorry to worrie you with this Mr. President but hard as it is to believe the releaf officials here are using up most every thing that you send for them self + their friends. they give out the releaf supplies here on Wednesday of this week and give us black folks, each one, nothing but a few cans of pickle meet and to white folks they give blankets, bolts of cloth and things like that. I dont want to take to mutch of your time Mr president but will give you just one example of how the releaf is work down here the witto Nancy Hendrics own lands, stock holder in the Bank in this town and she is being supplied with Blankets cloth and gets a supply of cans goods regular this is... one case but I could tell you many.

"Please help us mr President because we cant help our self and we know you is the president and a good Christian man... Yours truly cant sign my name Mr President they will beat me up and run me away from here and this is my home."

lose their jobs when times grew hard and often the last to receive federal relief.

1. AFRICAN AMERICANS

Black Americans had little reason to be optimistic about Roosevelt's election. Many still saw the Democrats as the party that supported white superiority and segregation; Roosevelt himself had done little to support the black cause. Now, having to work with a Southern-dominated Congress, he deferred to Southern attitudes on race. He failed to support an antilynching law, for example. Although black unemployment was as high as 50 percent in 1932, and Hoover was widely blamed for the economic crisis, more than two-thirds of black voters still supported the Republicans in the 1932 election.

By the early 1930s the economic advances achieved by African Americans after World War I had been wiped out. More than half the employed African Americans were concentrated in domestic service and farming, both of which offered unstable and often merely casual employment.

A plantation owner's daughter checks the weight of cotton in Kaufman County, Texas, 1936. The plantation system depended on cheap black labor.

TENANT FARMERS

Most Southern blacks were tenant farmers or sharecroppers who, like poor whites, eked out a livelihood on worn-out single-crop fields, growing mainly cotton. Their diet was mostly cornbread, molasses,

The Scottsboro Boys

When thousands of young people took to the rails hitching rides on freight trains in search of work, they were joined by many of the black youths escaping the deflated economy of the South. It was this catalyst that brought about one of the most notorious racial injustices of the entire Depression, and perhaps of all times.

The Scottsboro Boys (named after the Alabama town where they were tried for the first time) ranged in age from 13 to 21. Of the nine young black men, five were from Alabama and four were from Tennessee. On March 25, 1931, they hitched a ride on a freight train bound from Chattanooga, Tennessee. During the journey they became involved in a fight with some white boys on board the freight car they were riding. The black boys were forcibly removed from the train by a sheriff's gang at Paint Rock, Alabama, and charged with raping two white mill workers, Ruby Bates and Victoria Price. The women, who were also on the same train, had made up the story to avoid being arrested by the police: They had been in trouble for minor misdemeanors before. By the end of the month eight of the nine boys had been convicted and sentenced to death.

The obvious lack of evidence in the case generated an enormous amount of publicity, which reached far beyond the borders of the United States. An international petition of intellectuals and scientists (including Albert Einstein) demanded the release of the convicted boys, but to no avail. They were convicted by an all-white Alabama jury, despite the fact that an exposé by the *Daily Worker*, only days after their arrest, revealed that the whole incident had been a frame-up.

The day after they were sentenced to the electric chair there was a large demonstration at St. Luke's Hall in Harlem, New York. The following week the communist-backed International Labor Defense joined the parents to find a new attorney to lead an appeal. They appointed New York attorney Samuel Leibowitz, who demolished the case on its lack of evidence and on Ruby Bates's confession that no rape had taken place. Again the jury imposed the death penalty. The Supreme Court overruled the judgments in 1932, but Alabama officials refused to drop the case.

The lengthy judicial proceedings involved several more trials and ended with five of the boys being sentenced to long terms in jail, while the remaining four had the charges against them dropped in 1936. Four of the five were paroled in 1950; the fifth had escaped from jail in 1947 and fled to Michigan, where the governor refused to surrender him to the Alabama authorities.

Poster advertising a defense meeting in support of the Scottsboro Boys, accused of raping two white girls in Alabama.

Mary McLeod Bethune

Born into a farming family in South Carolina in 1875, Mary McLeod Bethune played an important role in improving the lives of African Americans. She taught at Haines Institute in Augusta, Georgia, and resolved to focus the rest of her life on the education of African Americans. Following her marriage, she moved to Florida, where she founded the Daytona Normal School and Industrial Institute for Negro Girls. She was also the founder of the Bethune-Cookman College and actively supported a hospital and other municipal facilities for black people.

The Depression led Bethune to believe that politics was the way to remedy black poverty. In 1935 she formed the National Council on Negro Women, and the next year she became a director of the National Youth Administration's Division of Minority Affairs. As leader of the "Black Cabinet" of federal officials, Bethune used her access to Roosevelt to push him to make the New Deal more sensitive to the issue of race.

Mary McLeod Bethune at a National Youth Administration meeting. Her friend and supporter, Eleanor Roosevelt, stands beside her.

effectively undermined previous forms of tribal government and left many former Native American lands open to white settlement. By 1933, 90 million of the 138 million acres occupied by Native Americans when the act was passed were surrounded by white holdings. This fragmentation contributed to the gradual break-up of tribal life, but without the alternative of integration into the white community. Native Americans often lived on infertile land in communities rife with trachoma, tuberculosis, and other diseases.

Their agriculture was frequently devastated by grasshopper infestations and drought.

FEDERAL SUPPORT
As president, Herbert Hoover had been interested in and sympathetic to the plight of the Indians. Although in the early years of the Depression he had reduced government expenditure, Indian communities had actually received an increase in federal aid. Roosevelt, who admitted that he knew little about the subject, was happy to take advice from

Secretary of the Interior Harold Ickes and John Collier (see box, page 38). In 1933 he appointed Collier as commissioner for Indian Affairs. A longtime advocate of Indian rights, Collier had previously led the militant Indian Defense Association.

Tribal Self-Government
In 1934 Collier—with the help of Nathan Margold and Felix Cohen, two attorneys from the Interior Department—succeeded in enacting the Indian Reorganization Act (RA), otherwise known

as the Wheeler-Howard Act. Although its original provisions were watered down during its passage, the act nevertheless provided for a return to tribal self-government and forbade the further allotment of tribal lands to individuals. Tribal members could sell their land, but only to the tribal group. In this way the act prevented the further erosion of Native American property by whites, though it did nothing to rectify the checkerboard pattern of Indian land holdings.

The act also set aside up to $10 million credit to fund Indian business and community ventures and provided funding for American Indian students who wished to pursue further educa-tion. Suddenly, for the first time, native peoples were given the chance to purchase, manage, and sell property, to have their own government, and to engage in business enterprise. They were also granted the right to self-govern-ment and democratic process.

Some 174 native tribes and groups approved the act; 78, how-ever, rejected it. A total of 92 tribes actually went on to adopt constitu-

tions. Those Native Americans who rejected the deal or refused to adopt constitutions did so either because they had become relatively prosperous without their own tribal governments, or because they argued that the RA's "democratic process" and elected tribal governments were an imposition of white values on Native American society. The failure of numerous tribes to adopt

An Apache family outside their wickiup on San Carlos Indian Reservation, Arizona, 1939.

the act provided ammunition for opponents of reform to resist further change.

EDUCATION

Before the New Deal the government's approach to educating Native American children had been rigid and unsuccessful. Children were often taken by force from their homes, put into schools—often boarding schools—and subjected to harsh discipline and standardized courses of study. Their routine devoted half their time to schoolwork and half to institu-tional tasks such as laundering, cleaning, wood chopping, and food preparation. A lack of funds meant that living conditions and standards in the schools were dangerously low. The children were forbidden to speak in their own language while in school and thus lost touch with their families and traditional tribal life. As a

Eyewitness Report

Author Alden Stevens wrote about the plight of a tribe of 700 Indians in southern New Mexico in his book *Wither the American Indians?* He described them "living in dilapidated tents, brush tepees, board shacks. Like hungry sparrows hoping for a crust of bread, these once proud people depended on their harassed agent to keep them somehow from starvation....

"Living on a reservation rich in natural resources and potentialities, they had never been taught or allowed to manage their own affairs. Instead, the Indian Bureau had handled—and mishandled—everything for them. Inevitably this tribe...had become shiftless hangers-on at the agency, diseased, discouraged, broken in spirit."

result, they ran the risk of returning home as dissatisfied misfits, unable to readapt to reservation life and equally unable to find a place in the white community. Although they had learned to read and write, they were unfamiliar with the customs and language of their own people. Their schooling did little to prepare them for earning a living among either Native Americans or the white population.

Education Reforms

The new program recognized that the attempts to remove children from their families and tribes in order to "civilize" them had failed. The New Deal, therefore, provided the children with a basic

John Collier, commissioner for Indian affairs, meets Blackfoot Indian chiefs in Rapid City, South Dakota, 1934.

Government Loans

Congress had allocated $10 million as loans to help the newly formed local tribal governments start up. The repayment of these loans went into a revolving fund, which was then made available for new loans. Different tribes used the loans to set up financial enterprises ranging from trading posts to livestock cooperatives. The system seemed to work far better in small, close-knit tribes. On the larger reservations greater distances between groups of people caused mutual distrust and jealousy within the various communities, which, in turn, hampered cooperation.

education without taking them away from their families. Along with reading, writing, and math they were taught hygiene and mechanical skills.

Education now took place in day schools on the reservations. The old boarding schools were used principally as vocational and trade schools. Some of them were also accredited by higher institutions, which meant that a few Native Americans were able to go on to higher education, mostly at state universities. As time went on, more and more Native Americans were taken onto teaching staffs in schools.

Since Indian land was exempt from taxation, the government paid a small tuition fee to the school district for each pupil. The act was the first time Native American education had been successfully addressed. For the first time, too, adult Native Americans took a real interest in the academic education of their children, in some cases even getting together to find an adequate building to serve as a school in their community.

EMPLOYMENT

The majority of Native Americans were, as they traditionally had been, subsistence farmers. Those who were semiskilled or skilled workers tended to be concentrated in the fishing industry in the Pacific Northwest and in lumbering operations in Oregon, Montana, Arizona, Wisconsin, and other states.

In the Southwest a new source of income developed through the sale of tribal arts and crafts. This occurred particularly among the Navajos, who became famous for their woven blankets and jewelry, and among the Pueblos, who were admired for their beautiful pottery. In 1936 Congress set up the Indian Arts and Crafts Board to provide the tribes with aid in marketing and to ensure the quality standards for each type of craft product. The manager of this board, René d'Harmncourt, put together a magnificent show of Indian products and culture at the Golden Gate International Exposition in 1939.

Low Incomes

Despite such initiatives, the incomes of Native Americans continued to languish in the lower third of the scale for all workers in the United States—the average income for a family of four in 1937 was just $600. Much of this revenue came as work relief or direct government relief. In addition, 40 percent of Indian children over 10 years of age were working, half of them as unskilled laborers.

HOUSING

Housing was a severe problem in any area where there had been white penetration into the Indians' traditional homelands. Only those communities that had escaped the destructive effects of the Allotment Act had fared reasonably well. The best housed of these were the Pueblos of New Mexico and Arizona, who dwelt in sturdy terraced homes on the hillsides, made from stone or adobe. On the plains, however, Native Americans fared far less well. Many of them were nearly landless, virtually penniless, and had no way of making a living. Unlike the Pueblos, they had no natural building materials with which to construct durable homes. Plains dwellers and their forebears had for years survived the winters in dirt hovels and tar-paper shacks.

A Navajo woman weaves a rug on a large wooden loom. Traditional arts and crafts were an important aspect of Native American tribes' cultural identity. Partly aided by federal initiatives, the sale of these arts and crafts also became a useful source of revenue.

The federal Indian Office received support and finance from the Reorganization Act and the Farm Security Administration to provide new housing for Native Americans. Most of the construction work was done by the Native Americans themselves, improving employment opportunities. Even with this help, however, the housing situation for most Native Americans remained inadequate.

HEALTH IMPROVEMENTS

Health and disease had also been a longtime problem for the Native American population, with tuberculosis and trachoma taking a heavy toll. Among common infant diseases were intestinal disorders, measles, whooping cough, and various skin conditions. However, with improvements in diet and shelter, along with a growing acceptance of Western medicine, Native American resistance to such diseases gradually improved.

HANDING OVER RESPONSIBILITY

The RA had been designed to pass on the responsibility for the running of the social services it established to the tribes themselves once they proved capable of handling that responsibility themselves. In this way the Indian

Poster for the Indian Court exhibit at the Golden Gate International Exposition, San Francisco, 1939.

Office intended to withdraw gradually as the native peoples became more self-sufficient. At the same time, Native Americans were trained and encouraged to seek government positions within the Indian bureau to contribute to the welfare of their own people.

3. MEXICAN AMERICANS

After the Mexican-American War of 1846–1848 many Mexican Americans lived on land granted to them by the Mexican government. They generally remained

Terraced Pueblo houses in New Mexico, 1939. The Pueblos tra- ditionally used local stone or adobe to build strong, durable houses that were several stories high.

there for many years. However, the influx of Anglo settlers in search of land on which to raise crops and livestock caused the demand for land to increase. Mexican American landowners now had to legally justify their claims under U.S. law. This process was expensive, and many had to sell large tracts of their land to pay off loans they had incurred. Language barriers sometimes inter- fered with a clear understanding of the property laws, and many Mexi- can Americans were cheated out of their land. By the late 1800s most Mexican Americans had become tenants or workers on land owned by Anglo Americans. The large migration of Mexican laborers came later.

ORIGINS OF THE MIGRANT WORKERS

During the early 1900s the economic situation in Mexico began to decline, and many Mexicans migrated north looking for work. Then, in 1910 the outbreak of the Mexican Revolution signaled the start of years of political and economic chaos. This revolution triggered the mass immigration that continued until the 1930s.

Between 1910 and 1930 more than 680,000 Mexicans came to live in the United States. During the 1920s Mexicans accounted for more than 10 percent of all U.S. immigration. Most settled in the Southwest, where they took laboring jobs on farms and ranches, as well as on railroads and in factories.

Immigration Restrictions

Immigration restrictions and growing discrimination began to take their toll on Mexican immigration even before the Depression. In 1917 the United States passed a law requiring all

Collier Critics

John Collier (1884–1968) was much criticized for his work in aid of the Native Americans. He was accused of communism and of trying to do too much too soon, which the tribes themselves resented. He was also described as a sentimentalist who wanted to hold the Native Americans back for the benefit of tourists and anthropologists. Added to these criticisms were individual complaints about the superintendents and other officials involved in the program. In truth, many problems were not resolved, and perhaps there was little chance that they could have been. Worst of all, nothing was done to maintain tribal traditions, which led to a society wracked by alcoholism and, in many cases, virtually destroyed.

control illegal immigration across the Mexican-U.S. border. There was also pressure from groups such as the American Federation of Labor and state farm bureaus to restrict the number of Mexican Americans entering the United States to protect jobs.

In the 1930s discrimination against Mexican Americans became much worse. They were often seen as a drain on the American economy because they held many low-paying jobs, while other, Anglo-Saxon Americans went unemployed.

SEASONAL WORK
Although there was a seasonal influx of Mexican workers during the harvest season into the southwest of the United States— in particular to California's San

This family of poor Mexican sugar-beet pickers, who had moved up from Texas, was sharing one small room in East Grand Forks, Minnesota, in 1937.

adult immigrants to be able to read and write at least one language, and in 1924 the U.S. Bureau of Immigration established the Border Patrol to

Joaquin and Imperial valleys—not all these migrants came from Mexico. A portion of them were year-round residents of the United States. They lived and worked in a wide variety of occupations, finding jobs in packing houses and at various other factories in the region, such as the food-processing plants of Heinz. They also worked on the construction of the railroads when such work was available.

Because the Mexican workers were not specialized, it was often necessary for them to move around in search of work. Due to the innate seasonality of their labor, they were among the first to suffer when the Depression hit. In the early 1930s, as they lost their jobs to impoverished white workers, hundreds of Mexican workers were literally stranded in Los Angeles, while county officials and politicians looked for ways to be rid of them. These officials reflected administrative policy all over the country toward non-Americans. Hard times, they felt, made it imperative that available jobs and resources should be reserved for white American citizens.

DEPORTATION

During the Depression hundreds of thousands of Hispanics, including many U.S. citizens, were informally deported by local communities, employers, and state governments. This was a reaction to the perception that there were not enough jobs available for Americans, let alone people from outside the United States.

The Mexicans were considered among the easiest Hispanics to get rid of since they formed a sizable group and came from a country sharing a border with the United States. The few living in the Midwest who managed to keep their

jobs survived on two or three days' work each week.

Government policy was to encourage people to return voluntarily to their supposed homeland, but thousands were deported against their wishes. In Santa Barbara, California, immigration officials herded farm workers into sealed boxcars to carry them to Mexico. Many of these immigrants considered the United States their homeland, having lived here for over 10 years. In addition, their American-born children were often U.S. citizens. Of the roughly three million people of Mexican

A Mexican woman cooking tacos at a stand in the Mexican quarter of Los Angeles. Mexican Americans had started to move into the cities of the Southwest during the 1920s, when they set up home in neighborhoods called colonias.

descent living in the United States in 1930, about half a million had been repatriated by 1939.

GENERAL DISCRIMINATION

In addition to the humiliation of repatriation, or deportation, Mexican Americans suffered other forms of discrimination. In many areas restaurants refused to serve them, while public places such as swimming pools, restrooms, drinking fountains, and movie theaters were often segregated. Mexican American schoolchildren were often forbidden to speak Spanish in the classroom and were punished for doing so.

Most Mexican Americans did not qualify for relief. The appearance of their name on the welfare lists that decided who could and could not receive relief was a cause for deportation. Many states and cities, meanwhile, allowed only "genuine" U.S. citizens to work on public works projects. Even the Works Progress Administration gave preference to U.S. citizens.

The Hoover administration began the policy of deportation after the stock-market crash of 1929. The policy was continued by Roosevelt, although fewer people were repatriated. In addition, Hoover applied strict new restrictions on Mexican American immigration. During the thirties the number of legal immigrants from Mexico was only 23,000, compared to more than 480,000 in

Employment Records

Employment records for the Depression years often left out Mexican Americans. Due to the itinerant nature of their jobs and life styles, and the often illegal nature of their migration, many were not accounted for in any census of the period. The fact that they were migratory made their numbers difficult to assess.

the previous decade. Generally, however, far fewer immigrants were arriving, mainly because of the poor economic prospects.

The National Industrial Recovery Act and the Agricultural Adjustment Administration were established to help mainly large interests in industry and agriculture, not migrants. The Wagner Act, intended to strengthen labor unions, did not apply to migrant agricultural workers. Even the Social Security Act did not cover farm laborers. The Farm Security Administration did concern itself with some problems of migratory workers; but by the time it was implemented, many Hispanics had already been displaced.

4. IMMIGRANTS FROM EUROPE AND THE EAST

In the late 19th century there had been an influx of Chinese and Japanese immigrants to the West Coast, mainly California. At the time these immigrants met a real need for labor in the far west, especially on the railroads, which were then under construction. During the early 20th century, long-standing prejudice against Asians intensified as Asian workers became a perceived threat to white jobs. Large-scale social and economic discrimination began. Laws were enacted, for example, to prohibit immigrant Japanese from owning land.

FILIPINOS
Many Filipinos had emigrated from the Philippine Islands to Hawaii and California during the 1920s. This migration posed problems, since no regulation of Filipino immigration existed—the islands were a U.S. possession and thus not covered by immigration legislation. The indiscriminate influx led to antagonism, violence, and discrimination as labor organizations and "patriotic groups" argued that the Filipinos

A row of basic houses in the Mexican section of San Antonio, Texas, 1939. Like blacks, Mexican Americans lived in segregated housing.

Mostly European immigrants crowd the Brooklyn Post Office, New York, in 1940 as they prepare to register for U.S. citizenship.

protect American workers from foreign competition. However, the protection did not extend to all workers in the United States. There was indeed equality for some, but the vulnerable minorities continued to suffer the most.

took American jobs. Finally, in 1934 Congress created an immigration quota that restricted Filipino entrance into the United States to 50 persons per year.

EUROPEAN IMMIGRANTS

Few non-Anglo-Saxon Americans were treated as equals right away in their new land, although most fared better than the ethnic minorities already mentioned. Generally, European immigrants over the years had been assimilated into American society and had adopted, to some extent, American cultural mores. This immigration had been encouraged in the late 19th and early 20th centuries, when it met a desperate need for unskilled labor in the mines and mills of a booming

A family of wealthy Jewish immigrants who have fled the Nazis in Danzig, Germany, arrive in Hoboken, New Jersey, in 1938. Armed with a $100,000 credit note, they hoped to find some land to settle in southern California. Between 1933 and 1944 Jewish people comprised one-third of all immigrants to America.

economy (see Volume 1, Chapter 1, "The United States, 1865–1914"). Many Europeans went on to become farmers, with large numbers settling land in South Dakota, Minnesota, western Iowa, Nebraska, Kansas, and Texas.

THE UNITED STATES CLOSES ITS DOORS

With the onset of the Depression the Hoover administration strictly enforced immigration restrictions passed in the 1920s in order to

SEE ALSO

◆ Volume 1, Chapter 1, The United States, 1865–1914

◆ Volume 1, Chapter 7, Hoover: The Search for a Solution

◆ Volume 2, Chapter 5, Where Did the Depression Bite?

◆ Volume 3, Chapter 2, Shadow over the Countryside

◆ Volume 4, Chapter 2, The Supreme Court

3

SOCIETY IN THE 1930S

Just as the previous decade, the so-called "Roaring Twenties," had affected every level of American society differently, so the Great Depression changed people's lives in a variety of ways. For those at the upper end of the scale daily life barely changed; for those lower down it altered beyond recognition.

The Great Depression did not affect all of society equally. Although the popular understanding of the thirties conjures up images of dispossession and poverty, some Americans found that their standard of living improved over the decade; for huge numbers, however, life changed for the worse. Collectively, the arrival of mass poverty following a period of

great prosperity in the United States was to have a profound affect on the American psyche.

1. THE DEPRESSION AND SOCIAL CLASS

The Americans least directly affected by the Depression were the rich. When the stock market crashed, few lost all of their money; most had investments spread across a wide portfolio.

Picnickers enjoy a day out in Wildwood State Park, Long Island, New York, in 1936. The new state and national parks were popular vacation destinations.

The crash did rob the wealthy of some of the respect they had been accorded as leaders of U.S. society. At the start of the 1930s, however, the richest 5 percent of Americans still controlled three-

This late 1930s lady's hairstyle is modeled on the Edwardian style of decades earlier. While others economized, rich ladies continued to follow the latest fashions.

quarters of the entire nation's wealth. Although the wealthy complained during the 1930s about Roosevelt's tax hikes, in reality the tax burden did not increase massively. In 1936, for example, the tax on an income of $1 million rose by only $1,800, or one-fifth of 1 percent.

The twenties' parties that F. Scott Fitzgerald described in *The Great Gatsby* (1925) continued in the thirties (see Volume 1, Chapter 4, "The Roaring Twenties"). Until Prohibition ended in 1933, the rich drank cocktails in each other's lavish apartments. Women continued to follow the latest fashions illustrated in magazines such as *Vogue* and *McCall's*. The Parisian style of long, flowing scarves, close-fitting hats, and low hemlines

For those who could afford it, travel could be luxurious. These wealthy young people are enjoying an in-flight diversion in spacious seating aboard a Pan American Martin Clipper in 1936.

was popular among wealthy women. As it became increasingly fashionable to escape cold northern winters for the southern sun of Miami, Florida, the Cuban capital of Havana, and the Caribbean, fashion magazines advised on the latest clothes for the trip. The glamorous fashion magazines were enormously influential. When *Vogue* announced, in 1935, that mink fur was the fashion item of the winter, fur sales boomed.

The rich lavished similar attention on their homes, furnishing them with antiques bought from economically depressed Europe. Europe's aristocracy sold family heirlooms to wealthy Americans who were delighted to acquire porcelain, antique silver, paintings, jewelry, and French furniture at competitive prices.

Lower prices for consumer items at home meant that the wealthy could buy things but spend less money. The paradoxical result was that sales of luxury items remained constant. General Motors, for example, suffered a decline in sales of the cheaper

Chevrolet, while sales of the more expensive Cadillac remained steady during the same period.

THE MIDDLE CLASSES

The professional urban middle classes were more affected by the Depression than the rich, and their situation was near desperate at times. How much they were affected depended on where they lived and what the main breadwinner did for work. Professionals such as doctors and lawyers saw their incomes drop by 40 percent between 1929 and 1933 because they were dependent on their clients' incomes. In 1936 the incomes of physicians remained 18 to 30 percent lower than in 1929, and lawyers' incomes had dropped by 18 to 38 percent.

Typists, clerks, and other white-collar workers all suffered salary cuts as business slowed. New York City's well-paid stenographers experienced a salary cut of over 50 percent, from between $35 and $45 a week to $16.

Teaching in schools and, particularly, colleges became a

Local stores such as Eagles, here in 1935 celebrating its 50th anniversary in Selma, Alabama, faced increasing competition from chain stores through the decade.

stable and highly desirable job, although teachers' salaries were often cut, too. The city of Chicago paid its teachers in tax notes, and then, in the winter of 1932 to 1933, it could not pay them at all. Probably the most secure employment was working for the federal government. Washington, D.C., had the strongest economy of any American town.

Many small businessmen—grocers, druggists, fuel dealers—found that once the New Deal reforms started to take effect around 1933, they could enjoy a small but stable income, low taxes, and appreciating assets. Some took advantage of low prices to invest in land or the stock market.

There was a new challenge to the primacy of the small business-man, however. Many blamed Roosevelt for the erosion in their status, but in reality competition came from changes in business. In 1930 Michael Cullin opened the

world's first supermarkets, the King Kullen chain of food stores. The greater variety and lower prices offered by the high-volume stores encouraged other food sellers to adopt a similar approach. Independent, specialty stores also came under pressure from an increasing trend toward the establishment of chain stores. By the end of the decade main streets everywhere were coming to resemble one another because they all contained the same stores.

THE URBAN POOR

The Depression hit hardest those who had least. By 1932, 28 percent of American families were without a single worker. A year later the average family income had dropped from $2,300 in 1929 to $1,500.

Factory and unskilled workers were used to seasonal unemployment, often being laid off for several months a year; but the length and extent of the Great Depression made it extremely difficult to cope with. Workers with few savings had nothing to fall back on when they lost their jobs.

Homeless families moved to

wherever they could find shelter. The luckier ones moved in with other family members; the most desperate resorted to living in caves and even sewer pipes. Early in the decade one million Americans were living in shantytowns mockingly dubbed Hoovervilles for the then president. In New York City many families lived in an abandoned reservoir in Central Park. The contrast between the homeless people and the half-empty, luxury skyscrapers that edged the park was strikingly stark.

Poverty affected the diet of the poor. They ate leftovers from restaurants, stale bread from bakers, or watered-down soup from soup kitchens. Truck drivers might spill a crate of oranges on New York City's Lower East Side and pretend not to notice: It was the only fresh fruit many people got to eat. In 1933 at least 29 people starved to death in New York City. Across the country 110 deaths were reported, largely of children.

Diet and Disease

Many Americans found themselves lacking fresh fruit and vegetables in their diet, and unable to afford meat or fish. The lack of a vitamin-rich diet led to disease, including some that doctors believed they had eliminated during the twenties. Adults were susceptible to colds, influenza, and pneumonia. Children, whose resistance was weaker, fared worse still. Inadequate nutrition led to diseases such as rickets, anemia, and pellagra.

THE RURAL POOR

Farm prices fell to record lows after the stock-market crash of 1929. Often, produce was sold for less than it cost to grow, if it sold at all. In 1933 in Illinois a bushel (56 pounds) of corn sold for only 10 cents. In general prices were about one-third of the precrash level (see Volume 3, Chapter 1, "Shadow over the Countryside").

Between 1930 and 1940 the rural population decreased by 20 percent as farmers were driven by debt and the dust storms of 1933 and 1934 to abandon their land and seek work in the cities. By 1940 around 3.5 million people had left the Great Plains. Some traveled to the great cities looking for work, others to California. Others became vagrants, wandering from place to place (See Volume 3, Chapter 3, "The Dust Bowl," and Chapter 4, "California in the 1930s").

MIGRANTS AND HOBOS

As many as 200,000 boys and young men became migrants, moving across America in search of work. Since most did not have cars, they hitched rides or rode illegally on freight trains. It was a dangerous game: In 1933 Union Pacific Railroad reported that freight trains had killed hundreds of hitchers, many of whom had fallen from moving wagons. Louis Banks traveled the trains looking for work: "Sometimes ten or fifteen of us would be on the train. And I'd hear one of 'em holler. He'd fall off, he'd get killed.... And then I saw a railroad police, a white police.... He shoots you off all trains...he would kill you if he catch you on any train."

Once the drifters arrived in a new city, finding work, accommodation, and food was not easy. They slept in campsites near the railroads or in rescue missions and city shelters, depending on charity for food and warm clothing. The most they could hope for were temporary jobs with low pay.

Camaraderie was often the only thing that made life bearable. One hobo remembered, "Black and white, it didn't make any difference who you were, 'cause everybody was poor.... We used to take a big pot and cook food, cabbage, meat, and beans all together. We all set together, we made a tent."

Hundreds of drifters would rush to a town on the rumor of work. In California many picked fruit and vegetables or worked in canneries. They earned no more than $400 a year, half what the state decreed necessary for minimum subsistence. Others, hoping to repeat the gold rushes of the 19th century, panhandled for gold.

2. HOME LIFE

The Depression had a profound effect on home and family lives. The middle and working classes

Who Were the Migrants?

As farmers left the land, Southerners tended to make for the industrial centers of the Northeast and Midwest, while many from the Dust Bowl headed for California (see Volume 3, Chapter 4, "California in the 1930s"). They were joined by many other unemployed: office and factory workers, whole families of blacks and whites, Mexican Americans, older people, young people, and children. A large number of migrants were boys—high-school graduates and college dropouts—unable to find their first job, who hoped to locate whatever work they could.

Unemployed men get free food at the America Soup Kitchen in Washington, D.C., in 1936.

found themselves adapting to a new set of circumstances.

The middle classes struggled to maintain the living standards to which they were accustomed. It was the woman's responsibility to try and make ends meet on an average income of $20 per week. Women devoted on average more than 60 hours a week to making their homes as comfortable as

A man is helped onto a moving freight car in Bakersfield, California. Every day during the thirties about 1,500 young men grabbed lifts on freight trains.

possible. First Lady Eleanor Roosevelt acknowledged: "It means endless little economies and constant anxiety for fear of some catastrophe such as accident or illness which may completely swamp the...budget." Practicing economies such as baking bread, preserving vegetables, taking in laundry, and dressmaking became commonplace.

In 1931 sales of glass jars, used for preserving fruit and vegetables, reached an 11-year high, while

sales of canned food—except condensed milk—dropped. When household appliances such as toasters or coffee percolators broke, they were not replaced. Sales of domestic appliances—with the exception of the refrigerator, which was still a novelty—dropped dramatically through the thirties as households economized in any way they could. Buying day-old bread

and relining coats with old blankets were just some money-saving tips. In the evenings families stayed in and cut down on their socializing to save money. They relied on their savings, paid bills late, and took out second mort-gages on their homes. In May 1933

the situation was so bad that middle-class families took to the streets in New York to protest the number of property foreclosures and to petition for assistance in meeting their payments.

HOMES AND HOMELESSNESS

By 1934 some 40 percent of homeowners in 20 major American cities had lost their homes. The availability of real estate created a new, cheap pastime for some Americans fantasizing about moving. One woman recalled how her family used to spend its Sundays in the Depression: "Every Sunday we used to go house hunting.... You'd get in the Model A...and go look at the houses. They were all for sale or rent. You'd go look and see where you could put this and where you could put that, and this is gonna be my room."

For workers, particularly migrants, housing conditions were

•

"Every Sunday we used to go house-hunting.... They were all for sale or rent."

•

grim. Whole families squeezed into one room and shared bathroom facilities with all the other families in the building. For landlords the thirties were a boom time since they could rent the same space to more people and earn higher rents. In such conditions disease spread easily. Perhaps the only positive consequence of the situation was the strong sense of community fostered by the migrants.

The Role of Women

In nearly four million of the approximately 30 million households in America in 1930 the role of financial provider was assumed by the woman—not necessarily through choice, but because the traditional bread-winner, the man, was unable to secure work. The service industries in which women traditionally worked contracted more slowly than male-dominated manufacturing industry. Although a Gallup poll showed that 80 percent of men did not want their wives to work for wages, ultimately they had little choice but to accept the situation.

In the 1930s around 25 percent of women worked. The total proportion of women in the workforce rose modestly throughout the decade. They found jobs as domestics, in the rag trade, nursing, doing clerical work, and teaching. There were still relatively few opportunities in the professions—the proportion of male teachers rose by 5 percent, pushing women out of some teaching jobs—but women were an increasingly visible force in politics. Frances Perkins (1882–1965), who trained as a social worker, was the first woman ever to gain cabinet rank when she became secretary of labor in 1933 (see Volume 4, Chapter 6, "The Unionization of Labor").

The majority of women, like Emma Tiller, worked as domestics or cooks, using self-taught skills: "I trained my own self to cook.... I never doubted myself in nobody's kitchen. Which always means I had a job. You felt this independent because you knew they needed you. That's why I studied to be a good cook."

Their pay was low—lower than that of men—but all across America women worked. In Berkeley, California, 40 percent of women worked outside the home; in rural Mississippi the percentage was even higher. Black wives were twice as likely as their white counterparts to work, because black male unemployment was higher than white male unemployment.

Most working women were single and under the age of 25. It was still not the norm for married women with children to work for wages—only one mother in 10 worked for money—but the number of married women working was increasing rapidly.

Mrs. Winston Roberts, wife of a wealthy industrialist, had never done a day's work until her husband died. His investments had been haphazard, and she was left with very little: "I had four half-grown children and not much to get along with." She went into the negligee business with a friend: "For a year, she and I were together. We made them and sold them. I could make wonderful clothes. I didn't learn it, I did it. I was never helpless."

A smartly dressed Red Cross nurse receives a warm welcome from this family of sharecroppers at their farm home in Arkansas. Nursing was one of the few occupations into which women were readily accepted.

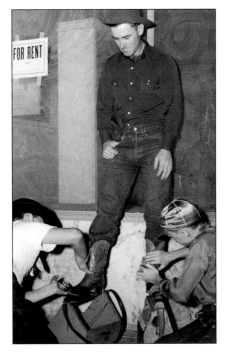

3. PSYCHOLOGICAL EFFECTS OF THE DEPRESSION

America's traditional reliance on hard work and individualism made it hard for people to accept that they did not have jobs. Success was seen as a result of individual effort; by the same

Above: A poor family in El Paso, Texas, victims of drought in the Southwest in 1931.

Left: Young boys shine shoes at a rodeo in Livermore, California, in 1939 to earn a little extra money for their families.

token, failure was interpreted as a sign of individual inadequacy. One common response to the Depression was that people blamed themselves, not the government, for their jobless status. Those with work looked on the unemployed as lazy reprobates who only had themselves to blame. One psychiatrist summed up the attitude he observed among those who lost their jobs: "Everybody, more or less, blamed himself for his delinquency or lack of talent or bad luck. There was an acceptance that it was your own fault, your own indolence, your lack of ability. You took it and kept quiet."

For many white-collar unemployed, claiming relief was an admission of failure (see Volume 4,

Chapter 5, "Welfare"). "I simply had to murder my pride," said one engineer, while an insurance man admitted, "We'd lived on bread and water three weeks before I could make myself do it." A 28-year-old teacher from Texas, who had lost her job after eight years, summed up the thoughts of many middle-class Americans affected by the Depression: "If...I can't make a living...I'm just not good, I guess."

THE FAMILY

Financial hardship had profound effects on the patterns of family life. Psychiatrist Dr. Nathan Ackerman studied the effects of unemployment on Pennsylvania miners who had lost their jobs. He found that the men spent their days hanging around the streets, reluctant to go home because their wives criticized and looked down on them. The men said their wives saw them as failures and made them feel guilty for not having work.

Ackerman explained how the women's frustration revealed itself: "The women punished the men... by withholding themselves sexually. By belittling and emasculating the men, undermining their paternal authority, turning to their eldest son. Making the eldest son the man of the family." Sons were often preferred to their fathers because they were younger, stronger, and could work harder. Most of the available jobs were filled by younger men, unskilled male labor at low wages.

As a result of the upheaval in their family relationships, many men suffered from depression. The only people who sympathized with them were their fellow unemployed workers. One jobless man described how he felt things had changed: "Before the Depression I wore the pants in this family, and rightly so. During the Depression, I lost something. Maybe you call it self-respect, but in losing it I also lost the respect of my children, and I am afraid I am losing my wife." Another man told how the balance of power had switched from him to his wife: "There certainly was a change…. I relinquished power in the family. I think the man should be boss in the family…. But now I don't even try to be the boss. She controls all the money…."

The change in the traditional family hierarchy had far-reaching effects throughout the decade. A survey in January 1934 of 64 cities revealed the number of families living with relatives varied from 2 to 15 percent. The highest percentage was in the South. Families that moved in with relatives had little privacy and found themselves confused as to who was in charge: Children found their grandmothers giving them one set of orders and their mothers another. Sons who had moved away from home when they started work moved back in with their parents and had to readjust to obeying their father's rules.

MARRIAGE UNPOPULAR
Pressure on family life meant that many couples postponed marriage indefinitely. The number of marriages fell by 25 percent over the decade. In 1929 there were 10 marriages per 1,000 people; that had fallen to 7.8 per 1,000 by 1934. The divorce rate also fell during this period, although historians believe that was because couples could not afford to pay for divorces. Instead, the number of desertions and couples living apart rose dramatically. By 1940 as many as 1.5 million married women were living apart from their husbands.

CHILDREN AND BABIES
Another effect of the Depression was a falling birthrate. In 1930 there were 21 births per 1,000 population; by 1933 this number had fallen to 18. Between 1935 and 1940 the annual growth in the number of births fell to zero. Many factors contributed to this decline. Couples may have had less sex because of tiredness or the emotional problems of unemployment. The fear of an unwanted pregnancy was itself a form of contraception. During the decade court decisions overturned much of the 19th-century legislation that made birth control illegal in many states. The Social Security Act (1935) funded states to set up birth control clinics, although strongly Catholic states did not do so; private organiza-

A farmer with his son in New Mexico in 1938. The eldest son often assumed the role of breadwinner if his father was out of work.

tions also promoted birth control. Condoms were more widely available. Gas stations had automatic condom dispensers, and drugstores also stocked them. Abortion was illegal in most states, women could often find a physician willing to carry out the operation. Risks were high, however: Many abortions were performed by unskilled practitioners. As many as 10,000 women died each year from botched operations.

WORKING CHILDREN
Many working-class families could not afford to raise their children. Between 1930 and 1931 the

An Oklahoma migrant, this house painter was left totally disabled by tuberculosis, one of the many diseases that became more common among ill-nourished Americans living in unsanitory conditions.

number of children placed in orphanages increased by 50 percent. By 1932 there were some 20,000 children in institutions whose parents could no longer afford to look after them. An estimated 200,000 children were living rough in America's cities.

Children who lived with their parents, meanwhile, were often expected to give up their education to earn money to contribute to the family's income. They found jobs shining shoes, selling newspapers, running errands, carrying groceries, mowing lawns, and collecting soft-drink bottles with a return value of two cents each.

Aaron Barkham had to quit school to work: "I never did get a whole year of school—maybe five or six months. I started working when I was 13. In a sawmill at 10 cents an hour." No concessions were made to his age: He worked the same hours as the adults. "Get up at four o'clock in the mornin' ....We started at a quarter to five and worked till we couldn't see. Then we'd quit. It was nearer sixteen hours than it was eight hours." Barkham spent his life working as a coal miner, lacking the education to do anything else.

THE OLD
Another increasingly vulnerable group of people were the old. Medical advances and an improved standard of living in the twenties had raised life expectancy to its highest levels yet. Many Americans were living longer: The number of people aged above 65 had risen from 4.9 million to 6.6 million over the decade.

The Depression hit the older generation particularly hard. Many had private pensions that were of little value after the stock-market crash, and only 28 states offered a state-funded pension. With payments that ranged from $7 to $30 per month, even they were not enough to live on. Older workers lost their jobs to younger workers, and unemployment among the over-60s rose to 40 percent. Many older Americans appealed to their families for help; but since family and friends were often also in economic difficulty, finding financial help was hard. The problem was particularly acute in California, where, in 1933, 20 percent of the population were over age 65, compared to the national average of 10 percent.

4. LEISURE TIME
Despite the gloom of the Depression years, Americans still managed to enjoy free time and

Unhealthy Children

Children often went without food: In New York City an estimated 20 percent of children were malnourished. In the coal-mining areas of Kentucky, Illinois, Ohio, Pennsylvania, and West Virginia, 90 percent of children were underfed. Writer Erskine Caldwell recorded a particularly shocking case where three sharecropper families shared two rooms in Georgia. A skinny six-year-old boy licked the discarded wrappings of a meat package, while "on the floor before an open fire lay two babies, neither a year old, sucking the dry teats of a mongrel bitch."

Black Americans

Few hardships were as acute as those experienced by America's ethnic minorities (see Chapter 2, "Equality for Some"). Native Americans, African Americans, and Mexican Americans suffered greatly from economic hardship coupled with entrenched racism.

Unemployment among black Americans was always higher than among whites. In the cities black unemployment ran at 30 to 60 percent higher than white unemployment. The average annual income for a family of four was estimated by the Works Progress Administration to be $973. In Chicago only 30 percent of black families earned that much; a third earned less than $500. In the South cotton-pickers earned on average only 60 cents a day.

Many of the semi- or unskilled nonrural jobs traditionally undertaken by blacks—cooks, maids, chauffeurs, bellhops, elevator operators, garbage collectors, and hospital attendants—disappeared when the Depression hit. Alternatively, employers preferred to give available jobs to whites first. In industries that employed high numbers of black workers, such as coal-mining and construction, they were laid off in large numbers. Black women often became the family breadwinners, and more black women than white women worked.

There were numerous instances of desperate white men using violence to seize black men's jobs. On the Illinois Central Railroad whites attacked and killed 10 blacks to take their jobs as firefighters. Urban blacks fought back. They boycotted stores that refused to hire black workers in New York, New Jersey, and Illinois. In 1935 rioting erupted in Harlem, New York, which left three blacks dead and many blacks and whites injured following rumors that a storekeeper had beaten a young black boy to death for stealing a penknife set.

Documentary photographer Margaret Bourke-White captured these poor black unemployed in Louisville waiting in line for relief handouts during the floods of 1937. Their presence provides an ironic contrast to the message on the billboard behind them.

Comfort in Books

Reading provided a fairly inexpensive form of escapism, although some people considered books a luxury item they could no longer afford to buy. Borrowing from public libraries increased during the thirties—the American Library Association estimated that between 1929 and 1933, libraries attracted more than three million new visitors. Many came to borrow books, while others just wanted a warm place to sit during the cold winters. During the same period the publishing industry saw the number of new titles published fall from 250,000 to 100,000. Publishing houses tried all kinds of marketing techniques to boost flagging sales. In 1936 the Book-of-the-Month Club was started to stimulate hardcover sales. Particularly successful was the introduction of softback dollar reprints of literary best-sellers. Also popular were the 25-cent pocket books, introduced in 1939. Sold mainly at newsstands and in drug stores, they were reprints of literary classics and best-sellers.

Many people living in the Depression particularly wanted to read long books in which they could lose themselves for a few hours and forget their worries (see Chapter 6,

This book club poster was designed by the WPA Illinois Art Project. Book clubs were very popular during the Depression.

"Chroniclers of the Depression"). Historical novels with a heady mixture of adventure, romance, sex, and fighting were especially popular. *Anthony Adverse* (1933), a long story of the Napoleonic Era by Hervey Allen (1889–1949), sold half a million copies in two years.

The most popular and best-selling novel of the decade was written by a woman. Margaret Mitchell (1900–1949) had taken 10 years to complete *Gone with the Wind*, published in 1936 (see box, page 110). The story, set in her native Georgia during the 1860s, was an immediate success worldwide. A very long novel, it transported the reader into the lives of uprooted Southerners during the Civil War and gripped them with the loves of the heroine, Scarlett O'Hara, and her battles with the forceful Rhett Butler. The novel could be interpreted as a tale of courage winning over poverty and also of the overwhelming of traditional values by modernity, represented by new forms of commercialism. Readers in the Depression related all too well to such themes.

A mobile WPA library in the 1930s. Mobile libraries made reading material available even to poor, rural communities.

seven and eight million. It was published in foreign languages, and there was even a Braille edition. The magazine's phenomenal success can be attributed to its generality: Because it covered many different topics, the reader only needed to buy one magazine.

There was also a ready market for true-confession and romance magazines. Women's glossies and general science magazines were popular too. The first issue of *Superman* in 1939 was instantly popular: Americans loved the idea of a clean-cut hero defeating the evil villain. Magazine circulations held steady during the Depression.

Smoking was another habit people were reluctant to give up—they liked to relax with a cigarette and a magazine at the end of the day. Tobacco factories were kept busy. Cigarette production rose from 123 billion in 1930 to 158 billion in 1936.

THE RADIO

For many Americans evenings at home invariably meant listening to the radio. Radio ownership rose continually during the thirties. Even in the worst years of the Depression, between 1930 and 1932, people bought four million radio sets. At the start of the decade over 10 million families already owned a radio, and by its end that number had tripled.

Radio stations were unlicensed and not subject to federal regulation. This meant that any station could broadcast with anybody able to buy their own airtime. Influential figures such as Huey Long and Father Charles Coughlin used the radio for their political campaigning. Advertising was used from the first days of the radio.

With the invention of the FM wavelength the number of stations grew. Major radio systems, such as

NBC (National Broadcasting Company), CBS (Columbia Broadcasting System), and the Mutual Broadcasting System, owned most of America's stations and broadcast across the whole country, helping create a national, rather than a purely local, identity. National broadcasts included soap operas, sporting events, and President Roosevelt's broadcasts. Roosevelt was the first

president to use the radio effectively, and his 16 "fireside chats" helped generate support for his New Deal policies. Americans in their living rooms heard the president explain his policies to them personally.

On average, each home listened to the radio for between four and five hours a day. Housewives listened to formulaic soap operas, so-called because soap and detergent manufacturers sponsored the 15-minute dramas. The daily episodes were packed with drama and action, providing the

listener with another form of escapism. One woman explained the soaps' attraction: "I can get through the day better when I hear they have sorrows, too."

In the late afternoon children's programs were broadcast, and in the evening the whole family would gather around to listen to the evening news and comedy shows like the long-running *Amos 'n' Andy* show (see Volume 1,

As part of the National Youth Administration program, young women from Illinois receive some tennis coaching on public courts. It was unusual for black people to play tennis, generally considered a white upper-class sport.

Chapter 4, "The Roaring Twenties"). Other popular shows included the husband-and-wife team of George Burns and Gracie Allen and adventure dramas such as the *Lone Ranger* and *Dick Tracey*.

Big-band music shows were popular evening entertainment,

UNDERWOOD & UNDERWOOD

Washington society women keep their figures in shape by playing medicine ball. Participation sports became more popular throughout all sections of society.

and on the weekends NBC would broadcast opera and classical music. The NBC broadcasts played a key role in widening classical music's appeal, and across the country the number of symphony orchestras grew. In 1940 New York's Metropolitan Opera appealed on the radio for help to ease its financial situation, and over $330,000 was sent by listeners. There was often more classical music than popular music on the radio.

RADIO HIGHLIGHTS
The huge influence radio exerted on its listening public is best illustrated by a notorious episode. On the night of October 30, 1938, Hollywood actor and producer Orson Welles (1915–1985), then aged only 23, broadcast an hour-long sketch based on H. G. Wells' story *The War of the Worlds* (1898).

Welles used the format of a newscast to vividly describe the invasion of the Earth by Martians. Equipped with death rays, the invaders terrorized New Jersey until they were killed by disease. More than a million terrified radio listeners panicked and fled their homes on foot or by car. One woman interrupted a church service in Indianapolis screaming, "It's the end of the world! You might as well go home to die. I just heard it on the radio." Welles had made clear at the beginning of the broadcast that a drama was

to follow, and three times the announcer had repeated that it was a dramatization, but such was the authenticity that many people took the story at face value. The next day Welles made an apology to the American public, but the power of radio had been established beyond dispute.

Radio was a great unifier during the thirties. Public events were shared simultaneously by the whole nation for the first time. The first national coast-to-coast broadcast was of the arrival of the transatlantic airship *Hindenburg*, on May 6, 1937. What was supposed to be a moment of triumph turned to disaster when the airship burst into flames, killing 36 passengers. Americans listened in horror to the voice of the commentator, Herbert Morrison, change from one of expectation to horror and shock as he described the explosion. The tragedy only increased the effect of the first national broadcast.

SPORTING LIFE
Sports retained their important role in American life, but in the thirties the emphasis in spectator sports shifted. Millions still listened to baseball games on the radio, and new stars like Joe DiMaggio (1914–1999) and Lou

The Hindenburg Disaster

The subject of the first coast-to-coast radio broadcast was the arrival on May 6, 1937, of the *Hindenburg*, a German airship. The previous year the airship had launched a commercial service between Germany and the United States. As the airship neared its mooring pylon at Lakehurst, New Jersey, the vast rigid, hydrogen-filled balloon burst into flames, and the airship fell to the ground. Of the 97 people on board, 36 died. The disaster was probably caused by electricity in the atmosphere reacting with a hydrogen leak. It marked the end of the use of airships in commercial transportation.

Gehrig (1903–1941) enjoyed devout followings. However, the continued dominance of the New York Yankees at the tail end of Babe Ruth's career dulled the excitement for many baseball fans.

College football was also badly hit by the Depression, too, because the game was too costly for many to follow. Instead, sports fans switched their attention to individual sports such as boxing and golf.

OUT AND ABOUT

The Depression galvanized the American public into action. Those who could afford it con-

tinued to attend games: Many of the country's sporting stadiums were built in the thirties. Those with less money listened to sports on the radio. Across the country, however, many Americans started to play sports for themselves. Under Roosevelt's government the Works Progress Administration built municipal swimming pools, tennis courts, and golf courses, and also donated $1 billion to new recreation areas, making sports more affordable.

Sports such as golf and tennis had declined in popularity between 1930 and 1934 since few people

public land, and private enterprises also constructed ski areas. The 1932 Winter Olympics, held in Lake Placid, New York, helped transform skiing from a practical activity into a pastime. Downhill skiing became all the rage as technological advancements introduced America's first ski lifts. Ski resorts in Colorado, Idaho, New York, and Vermont were established with ski schools. Road-

•

"It's the end of the world! You might as well go home to die! I heard it on the radio."

•

building and inexpensive train tickets made the country's mountain resorts easily accessible and cheap to get to, and helped start a national craze.

VACATIONS

Another craze was for summer vacations in the newly created state and national parks. In 1933 the National Park Service took control of lands that had previously been under the departments of War and Agriculture.

The CCC developed national parks, such as the Great Smokey Mountain National Park in North Carolina, which had fish and game reserves within national forests. There were also recreational areas, with picnic sites, cabins, and campsites. States worked with federal government to set aside land for public use. Between 1933 and 1936 more than 600,000 acres were turned into state parkland. Mississippi, Montana, Nevada,

Black sports hero Joe Louis (1914–1981), the "Brown Bomber," looks for an opening during a boxing match with the German Max Schmeling (1905–) in 1936. Schmeling, held up as proof of the supremacy of the Aryan race by Nazi leader Adolf Hitler, defeated the American. In a 1938 rematch Louis carried the hopes of a whole nation. This time he knocked Schmeling out in the first round, securing a victory not only for himself but, people felt, against Nazi racism.

could afford to pay club dues, but with the introduction of public facilities Americans rediscovered their love of sports. During the Depression they spent four times as much money playing sports as watching them. Swimming became very popular: More people visited their local pools than attended all spectator sports.

During the thirties Americans discovered winter sports, especially skiing and figure skating. The Civilian Conservation Corps (CCC) built ski runs and jumps on

The father-and-son team behind Kaunetz auto trailers, based on yacht-building methods, stand in front of one of their creations in Bay City, Michigan.

New Mexico, South Carolina, Virginia, and West Virginia all acquired their first state parks. In 1933 alone, California created seven new parks. Six million people visited the new state parks in 1934.

To get to the parks, many Americans drove. Car ownership increased as low fuel costs and cheap lodgings made road travel more attractive. Being able to keep a car was also often a matter of pride. With more leisure time, people invested in new auto trailers that offered a "home away from home." The trailers enabled a vacation on wheels, and a place to sleep meant savings on accommodation. In 1935, 35 million motorists took to the highways. By 1936, 50,000 trailers were being built each year; and despite a high price tag of between $600 and $700, they were briefly very popular. By 1938 the short-lived craze had passed.

The campsites continued to be popular. Those who did not have a car could travel to the parks by bus, the cheapest form of transportation. The railroads lowered their fares to compete; but once air-conditioning was introduced to the trains in the early 1930s, the railroads had the edge.

GAMBLING

As much as escape, another hope for many people was the possibility of a lucky win. Gambling was big business. With the lifting of Prohibition in 1933, thousands of taverns, amusement arcades, lodges, and clubs reopened. They needed something to attract cash-strapped customers through their doors and so installed pinball machines, slot machines, and punch boards. Slot machines, which were legal everywhere except the East Coast, were very popular because they were one of the few games that gave a money prize, returning 75 cents for every dollar spent. Bingo games were also popular because they were cheap—a bingo card sold for a penny—and offered useful prizes such as a ham or a new shirt.

Organized betting on horse races was legal in six states in 1929; by the end of the thirties that number had risen to 21. A 1938 poll found that more than half of all adult Americans had gambled in some form or another in the previous year. For many it represented the best chance they had of making a little money.

Fairs for the Future

Many popular recreation activities in the thirties were made possible through the publicly funded programs of Roosevelt's New Deal. Others were a result of improvements in technology. During the decade two major expositions, both showcasing the latest advances in technology, art, and industry, attracted large crowds—the Century of Progress International Exposition, held in Chicago (1933–1934), and the New York World's Fair (1939–1940). Twenty million people visited the Chicago exhibition, and more than 50 million attended the New York fair.

The New York fair cost $155 million to put on. It consisted of architecture and exhibits based on a "World of Tomorrow" theme. Built on swamplands in Flushing Meadows-Corona Park, which had been drained and landscaped, the site was dominated by two architectural structures—a trylon and a perisphere that enclosed a giant model of a future city. The Chicago exposition was sited on two parks off the shore of Lake Michigan.

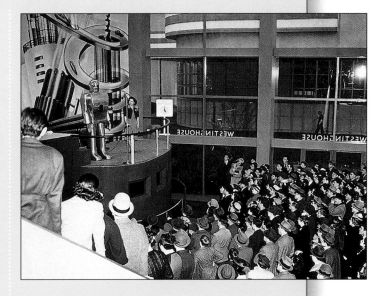

Crowds marvel at robots in the Hall of Electric Living at the 1939 New York World's Fair.

The crowds of visitors who flocked to these two imposing exhibitions were fascinated by the new products on show and also by updated versions of old products—from fountain pens to sponges and automobile steering wheels—which promised to improve their standard of living.

However, while they marveled at what the future held, many visitors failed to appreciate the irony of their situation. The technology that would transform their lives had already done so by making many workers redundant as mechanization transformed American industry—for example, the mechanical cotton picker and prefabricated housing increased unemployment in agriculture and construction respectively. Hundreds of factories lay empty while thousands of unemployed factory workers searched vainly for work. Productivity increased, but unemployment did not decrease.

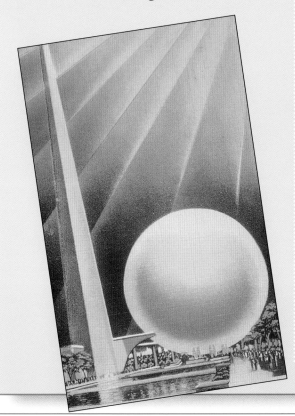

An artist's illustration shows the Trylon and the Perisphere, the futuristic structures built for the New York World's Fair.

THE ARTS IN THE DEPRESSION

The Depression played a major role in the development of the arts in the 20th century as American creators recorded the unparalleled events around them. Federal programs promoted public art and gave work to artists, writers, musicians, and actors. Such investment was partly a bid to restore a sense of national pride in the American people.

The first of Roosevelt's relief programs was the Civil Works Administration (CWA), which was in operation for six months in 1934. As part of the CWA the Public Works of Art Project (PWAP) came into being to create public art and to provide work for visual artists.

The idea of the PWAP had originated with George Biddle, himself an artist and old classmate of Roosevelt, who thought artists could be employed to stir national pride by their works. A similar program using muralists had already been successful in Mexico. Roosevelt supported the idea, as did Edward Bruce, a Treasury Department attorney and artist himself, who was subsequently placed in charge of the PWAP. Artists would provide paintings for a wide range of public facilities,

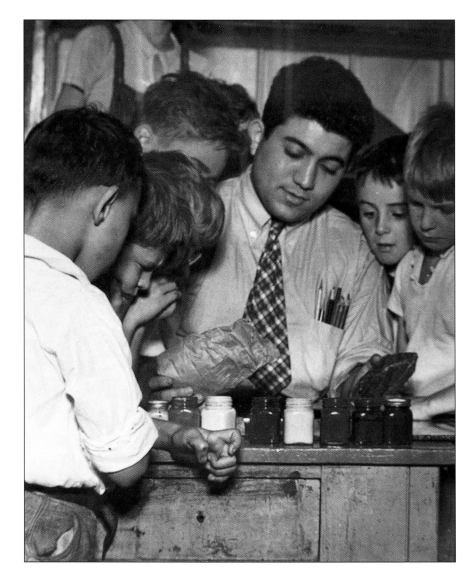

Children learn to mix colors at the Neighborhood House in Washington, D.C., 1935. The Federal Art Project provided free art classes for approximately 60,000 students—both adults and children—every month.

including public schools, orphanages, libraries, and museums. In 1934 the Department of the Treasury Section of Painting and Sculpture (later the Section of Fine Arts), again led by Edward Bruce, was established to place art in federal buildings.

Such programs recognized to an unprecedented degree not only the importance of arts and artists to society, but also their usefulness. Most previous government art had been patriotic statuary or portraits. At a time when the arts were widely considered elite luxuries, Roosevelt's funding acknowleged their potential for recording a momentous time and for shaping the spirit of all Americans.

1. THE WPA ARTS PROGRAMS

Despite the work of the CWA and PWAP, it was not until the Second New Deal that federal arts programs really began operating on a national scale. The Treasury Relief Art Program (TRAP) was founded in May 1935 to provide

•

Hopkins's retort was "Hell! They've got to eat just like other people."

•

murals and public art for federal buildings. At the same time, the Works Progress Administration (WPA) replaced the PWAP.

Headed by Harry Hopkins, the WPA oversaw programs ranging from construction to sewing. The WPA's Federal Project Number One, or "Federal One" as it was

known, was the umbrella for four cultural programs: the Federal Theater Project (FTP), the Federal Art Project (FAP), the Federal Music Project (FMP), and the Federal Writers' Project (FWP). Each had its own director and various regional administrators. The 1935 Emergency Relief Appropriation Act allocated $27 million of its $4,800 million budget to Federal One, and within a year about 40,000 WPA artists and craftspeople were working on arts projects across the country.

Critics attacked Hopkins and Roosevelt for supporting artists at a time of economic despair. Hopkins' blunt retort was "Hell! They've got to eat just like other people."

The WPA supported an explosion of creativity and a remarkable celebration of American life. Cultural expression in visual art, drama, writing, and music commemorated America's past, honored Roosevelt and the New Deal, and celebrated everyday life and the common citizen.

Proletarian ideals—concerned with ordinary working people— were a common theme connecting seemingly disparate arts. A rancher in rural Oklahoma or a small-town girl were as likely subjects for plays or paintings as presidents. Another important theme of arts programs was preserving and promoting the cultures of America's minorities, including African Americans, Mexicans, Jews, Native Americans, Appalachians, and others.

The WPA umbrella covered all forms of cultural expression, from fine arts and Shaker crafts to full-scale symphonies and blues field

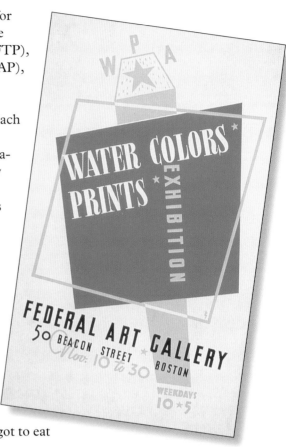

Poster advertising a WPA prints and watercolors exhibition at the Federal Art Gallery, Boston, Mass., in 1936 or 1937.

songs. The range and sheer volume of artistic endeavor were remarkable. Many artists were grateful for the opportunities afforded them and credited funding from the federal arts programs with enabling them to continue in their chosen profession.

A Conservative Approach

The WPA did not allow its artists full freedom of expression. They faced censorship and censure for expressing unpopular ideas as they questioned what American society should and could be. Edward Rowan, assistant director of the PWAP, had already expressed his feeling that while government artists should have "the utmost freedom of expression," the

A portable theater in New York, 1935. As part of the Federal Theater Project, productions toured around regional centers, bringing theater to the people.

subject matter of each project should be scrutinized. He added that "Any artist who paints a nude for the Public Works of Art Project should have his head examined." The PWAP also discouraged abstract or controversial art. Nevertheless, artists were generally unafraid of expressing their political and social views.

THE FEDERAL THEATER PROJECT (FTP)

In the Depression the theater suffered from both its patrons' lack of disposable income and competition from Hollywood with the introduction of the talkies (see Chapter 5, "Hollywood: The Depression Years"). In 1931 two-thirds of Manhattan's theaters shut. Staged live entertainment, especially vaudeville, was losing popularity and being supplanted

by new technologies such as phonographs, film, and radio.

In the 1929–1930 season Broadway staged 240 productions. The following season the number fell to 190, and eight out of every ten new plays failed. In subsequent years the number of productions halved. Thousands of actors and playwrights were laid off, along with many more backstage staff.

Established in August 1935, the FTP was designed to get unemployed actors and theater workers off the relief rolls and into work, and to bring the performing arts to the masses. Hallie Flanagan—a Vassar theater professor, classmate of WPA leader Harry Hopkins, and friend of Eleanor Roosevelt—was appointed to head the project. Regional centers were located in New York, Boston, Chicago, Los Angeles, and New

Orleans. New York City was the largest center, with 5,000 employees on its payroll in the early days. Among FTP participants who would enjoy later success were actor Burt Lancaster (1913–1994) and actor, director, and screenwriter Sidney Lumet (1924–).

The FTP employed about 10,000 people in total on a budget of $7 million. Pay ranged from $30 to $103.40 per month. It staged some 1,200 performances of classic and contemporary plays across the nation. By 1939, when the program was disbanded amid allegations that it encouraged pro-New Deal propaganda and the mixing of black and white performers on stage, total audience figures had reached over 30 million at a cost of around $46 million. Critic Howard Taubman called the period in the theater "the most

•

> *"Any artist who paints a nude for the PWAP should have his head examined."*

•

provocative and exciting…that this country has ever known."

The FTP came to national attention with the 1935 production by writer Sinclair Lewis (1885–1951) of *It Can't Happen Here*. Staged to open simultaneously in 22 theaters in 17 states on October 12, 1936, the play would run for

The Living Newspaper

The Living Newspaper, a subproject of the FTP, used a new combination of live performance with radio and newsreel techniques to create message-driven plays about contemporary issues. *One-Third of a Nation*, a performance about housing problems, was its most famous production. Productions also disseminated public health messages, as in *Spirochete*, launched to warn audiences about the dangers of syphilis.

260 weeks. Its success prompted famous playwrights of the day to follow Lewis's lead and permit their work to be performed royalty-free by FTP theaters.

The Living Newspaper

FTP productions had to entertain as well as educate. Vaudeville units toured Civilian Conservation Corps camps, and puppet shows delighted children in rural areas. Nevertheless, most FTP shows had a serious social message for the audience.

The Negro Theater Project

The largest and most infamous branch of the FTP was based in New York. The branch had six theaters, a magazine, a bureau for research and publication, and a Living Newspaper troupe. Orson Welles and John Houseman (1902–1988) were among its prominent employees.

Both Welles and Houseman became involved in the theater relief program through the Negro Theater Project (NTP), one of 16 such units in the nation designed to provide employment and entertainment for African Americans. The NTP mission was to perform plays by blacks for blacks, as well as classics with all African American casts. When Houseman joined the Harlem NTP in summer 1935, area unemployment was 80 percent, higher even than in 1933, when half of Harlem's residents had been on relief.

Houseman brought in Welles to assist the NTP with what he assumed would be African American source material. Instead, Welles had the idea of staging an African American production of *Macbeth* set in Haiti. The Harlem NTP's "Voodoo *Macbeth*" was the first FTP production (see box, page 64).

Project 891

Houseman wanted the FTP to serve as a springboard for a national American theater. He eventually asked to start a second company, Project 891, named for its governmental designation. The company included actors like Joseph

Poster for the Living Newspaper's most famous production, One-Third of a Nation, *at the Adelphi Theater. The production highlighted housing problems in the city slums.*

Cotten, Virginia Welles, Arlene Francis, and Jack Carter, plus other talented allies such as composer Paul Bowles (1910–1999), who later achieved fame as the writer of such works as the novel *The Sheltering Sky* (1949).

The Cradle Will Rock

The most notorious FTP production was one the project ultimately refused to stage. In March 1937 Hallie Flanagan approved a production entitled *The Cradle Will Rock* by composer Marc Blitzstein (1905–1964), an operatic drama set in Steeltown, U.S.A. Although Blitzstein's original theme had been prostitution, he had changed it—on the advice of fellow composer and playwright Bertold Brecht (1898–1956)—to include labor

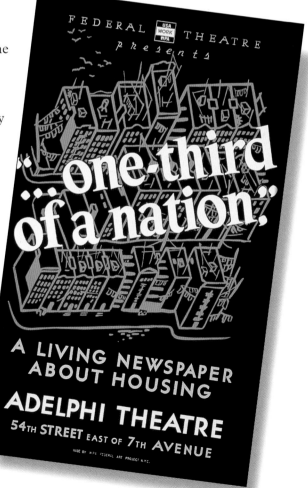

FEDERAL THEATRE presents

"...one-third of a nation"

A LIVING NEWSPAPER ABOUT HOUSING

ADELPHI THEATRE
54TH STREET EAST OF 7TH AVENUE

MADE BY WPA FEDERAL ART PROJECT N.Y.C.

Voodoo *Macbeth*

When the "Voodoo *Macbeth*" opened in New York on April 14, 1936, the curtain rose on a full house: Every one of the Lafayette Theater's 1,223 seats was occupied. In accordance with the FTP's requirement that a minimum 90 percent of employees come from relief rolls, 95 percent of the production's 130-strong all-black cast were amateur. Professional cast members included Jack Carter, Edna Thomas, and Canada Lee. Also included in the performance was a drum troupe from Sierra Leone, complete with witch doctor.

The idea of setting Shakespeare's classic in 19th-century Haiti, and using voodoo priestesses instead of witches, came from Orson Welles' wife, Virginia. Welles revised the text, changing the main theme from man being destroyed by ambition to man being controlled by supernatural forces. The new emphasis gave him the chance to use dramatic sound and lighting effects, a hallmark of his later plays and films.

Although *Macbeth* sold out a 10-week run at the Lafayette before moving downtown and then going on tour, it did not make money. It did succeed, however, in putting black people back to work and providing free or cheap entertainment for audiences who would otherwise have gone without.

The "Voodoo Macbeth*" opened on a jungle scene accompanied by the sound of beating drums.*

Other Theater

Not all theater was produced by the FTP. The Group Theater made its debut in New York in 1931. Its founders included actors who would become American stage luminaries: Lee Strasberg (1901–1982), Stella Adler (1901–1992), and playwright Clifford Odets (1906–1963). The Group staged work by new playwrights: Sidney Kingsley (1906–1995), Lillian Hellman (1907–1984), and Paul Green (1894–1981).

Other theater was produced under the New Theater League, the Playwrights' Company, Theater Guild, and as previously, by Broadway. Although trivial revues and lightweight musicals were common, social dramas also played on the commercial stage, including adaptations of John Steinbeck's *Of Mice and Men* (1937) and Erskine Caldwell's novel *Tobacco Road* (1932). *Our Town* (1938), a play by Thornton Wilder (1897–1975), was also a stage hit. It won a 1938 Pulitzer Prize.

problems. Now, the production coincided with labor strikes that began to break out in steel-producing areas in May 1937.

Meanwhile, the WPA faced budget reductions scheduled for June 16, 1937. Flanagan put a moratorium on new productions until the end of the fiscal year, June 30. The production of *The Cradle Will Rock* would have to be delayed, if it opened at all. The play was trapped in red tape: Conservatives did not consider strikes suitable material for art of any kind.

Advance ticket sales had been excellent, and the preview was planned for June 14. The day before, the WPA padlocked the theater. John Houseman and Orson Welles vowed to open the play and rented a different theater 21 blocks away. The actors' union refused to allow its members to perform at the new theater, so, when the curtain rose, Blitzstein, who was not a union member, sat alone at a piano. As Blitzstein performed, the actors sang their roles from their seats in the

audience. In all, the play played for more than 100 performances. These events, dramatized in the 1999 movie, *Cradle Will Rock*, marked the beginning of the end of the FTP.

The Demise of the FTP
The FTP, particularly the Living Newspaper, was a prime target for opposition to the New Deal that gathered strength after fall 1936. Harrison Grey Fiske, a *Saturday Evening Post* writer, accused the FTP of "disseminating communistic propaganda." Members of the FTP remained defiantly

Poster for Federal Theater Project staging of "It Can't Happen Here" by Sinclair Lewis (1885–1951). The play is about a future revolution that leads to Fascist domination of the United States.

leftist; many were prolabor, and some of them were communists. The project had made enough enemies on the right to be vulnerable. Representative J. Parnell Thomas of the House Committee to Investigate Un-American Activities launched investigations into claims of communist activity within WPA programs, beginning in Boston, New York, and San Francisco. Eventually, more than 1,500 workers were laid off. Theater leases ran out and were not renewed. *The Federal Theater* magazine was closed. Welles resigned, and Houseman was fired.

However, Welles and Houseman persevered. They launched Mercury Theater, which aired radio plays and eventually became the core group whom Welles would cast in his films, including *Citizen Kane* (1941) and *The Magnificent Ambersons* (1942).

Overhead view of the Rockettes on stage at Radio City Music Hall, the interior of which was designed by Donald Deskey.

dancing with Bill "Bojangles" Robinson on the movie screen was not high or serious art; it represented part of an emerging form of popular art, escapist entertainment. Until prosperity returned to everyday life, the popular arts in one form or another could be counted on to provide a diversion.

AMERICAN DESIGN

Decorative arts flourished in the Depression as the American public continued to be intrigued by design. Artists tried out new forms in architecture, interior decor, furnishings, and jewelry.

The style mainly associated with the era is art deco, which had originated in Paris in 1925. The style, sometimes called depression moderne, employed streamlined forms and geometric patterns created using industrial materials such as metals, plastics, and glass. Its popularity reflected the increasing role of industrial products in everyday life and the interest of artists and designers in the qualities of those products.

Streamlined Deco

In the later 1930s art deco became a sleek style associated with technology and speed, using smooth surfaces and glossy materials. It is called streamlined moderne or streamlined deco. Less decoration made designs easier and cheaper to mass produce. The style can be seen in the interior furnishings and fixtures of Donald Deskey (1894–1989), who used new materials—Bakelite, chrome-plated metal, linoleum, and glass bricks—in his design. So, too, did the popular Sears Roebuck Cold Spot refrigerator, designed by Raymond Loewy (1893–1986). These two designers are also notable for other icons of the era: Deskey, the interior of the Radio City Music Hall (1931), which featured art by Georgia O'Keeffe and Stuart Davis; and Loewy, the Coca-Cola bottle and packaging for Lucky Strike cigarettes.

In 1937 furniture makers Haywood-Wakefield introduced a line of home furnishings named Streamlined Moderne, the first mass-produced 20th-century furniture. The styles were repeated in popular entertainment, with Hollywood films often featuring luxe moderne interiors.

Organic and Industrial Design

In the mid- to late 1930s some American designers abandoned the stark angles of modernism for what they perceived as more organic forms. Enduring examples of this style are the chairs designed by Charles Eames (1907–1978). The chair, based on organic forms as well as the availability of new, highly flexible materials, became very popular in the early 1940s. It was mass produced by Herman Miller, Inc., in the middle of the decade.

Decorative arts were also heavily influenced by industrial design and architecture. New materials and changing ideas about where and how people lived led architects to explore new problems such as how to accommodate the automobile, for example, with "wayside markets" and innovative gas stations that could serve automobiles and aircraft alike. Popular architects who continued to be influential included Frank Lloyd Wright (1867–1959) and Buckminster Fuller (1895–1983), as well as European architects who immigrated to the United States in the late 1930s, such as Walter Gropius (1883–1969), Ludwig Mies van der Rohe (1886–1969), and Richard Neutra (1892–1970).

Depression Glass

Depression glass is the name given to utilitarian glassware made between 1920 and 1940. It was cheaply produced and often used as business premiums. Depression moviegoers could pick up dishes and glassware at "dish nights," where admission earned a free item. Frigidaire also gave away premiums to be used with its refrigerators.

Each item cost three or four cents to manufacture from cheap glass, brightly colored to hide any impurities. The glassware was produced in some 25 colors and almost 100 different molded patterns. Items varied from dinner plates to candy dishes, whiskey decanters, and lamps.

Poster for a 1941 WPA exhibit entitled "Index of American Design." Produced between 1935 and 1942, the exhibit included 18,000 detailed watercolors of decorative arts from colonial times through the 19th century. The project lent credibility and value to folk art, such as Shaker furniture and quiltmaking.

AMERICAN SCENE PAINTING

The term "American Scene Painting" is used to describe mainstream realist and antimodern painting styles that emerged during the late 1920s. Popular during the Depression, these styles are often referred to as "conservative," since the artists seemed to be reacting against modern and European influences. Two separate groups fall under the designation: American Regionalists and Social Realists. Some critics see the two as opposite sides of the same coin.

The American Regionalists, rather than being part of a formal school or movement, were rural, primarily Midwestern artists united by an interest in painting daily life in a nonmodern style. Most embraced realistic painting styles, which they used to explore contemporary society. Realists such as Andrew Wyeth (1917–), Reginald Marsh (1898–1954), and Alexander Brook (1898–1980) captured pastoral scenes from the American heartland.

Thomas Hart Benton, John Steuart Curry, and Grant Wood

(1892–1942) are the best-known regionalist painters. Benton at one time acted as an unofficial spokesman for the group. His family was political—his father and great uncle had been Missouri congressmen—and Benton sought to use art to support traditional and democratic ideals. These he believed could be embodied in depictions of rural America. Benton created several murals in Missouri at the state capitol and the Harry S. Truman Library. He is also known for having taught Jackson Pollock.

Curry, who also participated in the government mural projects, used rural Kansas as his subject. He was hired as artist in residence at the University of Wisconsin in 1937, the first such post granted at an American university.

Wood's interest in realism and American folk art can be seen most clearly in his famous *American*

Gothic (1930). The painting depicts his sister and his dentist as rural farm people, and it was this image that brought his work to national attention.

Social Realism
Social Realism was predominantly an urban, political style of art. Social Realist artists and intel-

Detail of a mural by Ben Shahn for the community building in Hightstown, New Jersey, 1938. Shahn is best remembered for his art depicting social issues.

lectuals strove to effect social change through their art. Although the movement was not entirely limited to the visual arts, Social Realist artists mainly made prints and drawings for pamphlets as well as art on larger canvases. Concentrated in the Eastern United States, these artists were inspired by magazine illustration and the work of the Mexican muralists, particularly Diego Rivera. Philip Evergood (1901–1973), Jacob Lawrence, Jack Levine (1915–), Paul Cadmus (1904–1999), and Ben Shahn

(1898–1969) are among those artists usually associated with Social Realism.

OTHER PAINTERS
Among the thirties' generation of painters only a few escaped being lumped into either the regionalist or realist groups, most notably Edward Hopper (1882–1967) and Charles Burchfield (1893–1967). Hopper's paintings were stark cityscapes populated, if at all, with solitary figures that evoked loneliness. Hopper supported himself as a commercial artist, painting signs and designing advertisements. His most famous work is *Nighthawks* (1942). Burchfield used watercolors to create "psychological landscapes."

About 1935 a marked change began in American art. Some critics see it as the end of the early modernist era, as artists embraced Abstract Expressionism. A small group of painters, many of them women or foreign-born Americans, explored this abstract style, which appealed to neither liberals nor conservatives. Arshile Gorky (1904–1948), Gertrude Greene (1911–1956), Willem de Kooning (1904–1997), Stuart Davis (1892–1964), and sculptor Alexander Calder (1898–1976) were among those closely associated with modern abstract art. At the end of the 1930s European exiles made their own unique contributions to the U.S. art scene. Among them were Hans Hofmann (1880–1966) and Josef Albers (1888–1976). By 1945 innovation and energy had made U.S. artists pivotal leaders on the international art scene.

3. NEW KINDS OF MUSIC
Between the late 1920s and World War II composers defined new forms of American classical and popular music. Many composers

ONE OF THE GREAT PRINCIPLES FOR WHICH LABOR IN AMERICA MUST STAND IN THE FUTURE IS THE RIGHT OF EVERY MAN AND WOMAN TO HAVE A JOB TO EARN THEIR LIVING IF THEY ARE WILLING TO WORK

who rose to prominence had studied in Europe in the 1920s, often under French music teacher Nadia Boulanger (1887–1979), but riches were also discovered in native music—folk, blues, and jazz—that had not before been taken seriously as art. Composers who worked with traditional music married it to classical structures or used it to create new musical forms heard in countless scores for musical theater, ballet, and film. The result was a vibrant, uniquely American music.

THE GERSHWINS

Composer George Gershwin (1898–1937) and his brother, lyricist Ira (1896–1983), have a legacy in both popular and classical music. They had strings of popular hits in musicals on stage and in film throughout the Depression. Many Gershwin tunes have become standards: "The Man I Love," "'S' Wonderful," "I've Got a Crush on You," "Nice Work If You Can Get It," and "Love Is Here to Stay." George combined jazz and gospel music with classical forms, most radically in the 1935 opera *Porgy and Bess*. Among his symphonic pieces are *An American in Paris* (1928) and *Rhapsody in Blue* (1924). Gershwin's influence was felt in both jazz and symphonic music.

COPLAND AND FRIENDS

One of America's most popular composers was Aaron Copland, whose music spanned classical, ballet, theater, and film. His 1938 book, *What to Listen for in Music*, helped popularize classical music; *Billy the Kid*, staged the same year, was a ballet that combined characteristic folk songs and western tales.

Copland also supported other composers, including Paul Bowles,

Marc Blitzstein, and Leonard Bernstein (1918–1990). From 1928 to 1932 the Copland-Sessions concerts brought to the public new chamber music by young composers. Copland also helped form, in 1932, the Young Composers Group, the members of which met at his home to discuss music. Notable members included Bernard Herrmann (1911–1975) and Oscar Levant (1906–1972), who said, "Copland has had a potent influence completely unknown to the public, in its sphere unmatched by that of any other native musician of the time."

Composer George Gershwin (left) and his brother, Ira, who wrote the lyrics for nearly all of George's songs.

More innovative experimental composers such as Henry Cowell (1897–1965) and John Cage (1912–1992) also began their musical careers during the 1930s.

JAZZ AND SWING

New jazz forms were being tried in centers such as Harlem and Kansas City. The Lindy Hop—named for national hero Charles Lindbergh—was a popular dance

Orchestral training for grade and high school students, 1934. The FMP's free music classes drew over 500,000 pupils a month, most of whom could never have afforded private tuition.

at clubs like the Savoy Ballroom, where dancers jived to swing music. By 1935 bandleader Benny Goodman (1909–1986) had risen to popularity with swing music for white audiences. Big bands were led by musicians such as Count Basie, Glenn Miller, and Cab Cal-

•

"Copland has had a potent influence completely unknown to the public…"

•

loway. Groups were usually split along color lines, although some band leaders, notably Goodman, made attempts to overcome them.

Tin Pan Alley, the hub of the popular music industry in New York, continued churning out popular tunes despite the economic gloom. The Hit Parade produced countless songs that became standards. In 1929 it was "Ain't Misbehavin'" and "Singin' in the Rain," and in 1930, "I Got Rhythm." Many songs of optimism became anthems of the day, like "Sunny Side of the Street" or "Who's Afraid of the Big Bad Wolf," from Walt Disney's cartoon *The Three Little Pigs*.

COUNTRY, BLUES, AND WESTERN

The thirties gave rise to new forms of popular music, much of it from the South. Artists such as the Carter Family and the Monroe Brothers interpreted traditional songs in distinctive styles. These country groups predated bluegrass, but were important influences leading to its eventual emergence in the 1950s.

So-called "race" records were popular. They were typically "city blues," as jazz was known, or "country blues" from solo artists, especially bluesmen like Charley Patton (1891–1934), Robert Johnson (1911–1938), and Son

House (1902–1988). Blues artists performed live in small clubs throughout the South and north to Chicago. From depressed areas where blue-collar workers were hit hard by unemployment, protest music spoke to conditions of the day. The genre included labor songs, many of which commemorated workers' heroism during particular strikes, and observations about social conditions. Popular artists included Woody Guthrie (1912–1967) (see box, page 117) and later Pete Seeger (1919–), who influenced a new generation of protest musicians of the 1960s.

Western music was also increasingly in vogue. The cowboy myth was at its height, supported by movie images and screen cowboys such as Gene Autry (1907–1998) and Roy Rogers (1911–1998). Bob Wills (1905–1975) and his band, the Texas Playboys, developed their own style of music, known as western swing.

4. POPULAR CULTURE

The 1930s saw an expansion of popular culture. Being current became highly important. Trends

Jazz musician Cab Calloway (right) was well-known for his flamboyant performances. His band enjoyed huge popularity in the 1930s.

European Influence

Classical music continued to have European influences. Many composers and musicians fled to the United States from Europe beginning in the 1930s, including Boulanger, Kurt Weill (1900–1950), Arturo Toscanini (1867–1957), Paul Hindemith (1895–1963), and Arthur Rubinstein (1887–1982). These artists had a profound effect on music until well after World War II.

Radio, meanwhile, began to broadcast the Metropolitan Opera in 1931. Programs such as Nashville radio station WSM's "Grand Ole Opry" were popular. Serial dramas had a loyal following.

Escapist as much of it was, popular art also informed and educated as much as it entertained. In that, it paralleled the populist beliefs behind the work of the WPA and its agencies.

and fads in song and dance were nothing new, but new media such as radio and film, and increased numbers of newspapers and magazines, made sure people heard about the latest films, songs, dances, and crazes far more quickly than before.

Popular culture reached the masses by the cinema and the radio. In 1939, 25¢ could buy admission to an afternoon at the movies plus two candy bars. Hollywood was at its most prolific. Technological innovation spurred filmmakers to experiment. When an American went to the movies, however, more than likely it was to see a genre film. Gangster pictures, musicals, slapstick comedies, and B-movies were extremely popular.

5

HOLLYWOOD: THE DEPRESSION YEARS

During the Depression going to the movies was a popular pastime for Americans wanting to escape for a few hours from the grim reality of their daily lives. Technical advances also contributed to the success of Hollywood's film industry in this period. New film genres, such as musicals and gangster movies, were able to exploit the new developments in sound.

Hollywood's importance was firmly established by the time of the Wall Street Crash. The film industry, centered in this California town where operating costs were low and the warm climate enabled films to be made all year, had expanded considerably during the 1920s, gradually spreading over a wide area of Los Angeles. A huge number of films were being produced at the end of the twenties, and crowds of hopefuls flocked to Hollywood from all over the country to seek fame and fortune.

The film industry was hit badly by the Crash. The fortunes of the film studios were initially rocked by the economic failures on the stock market, and most of them were instantly left in debt. In the years that followed, the studios struggled to find funding. Audience figures dropped sharply in 1931 and reached a weekly low of

Clark Gable, seen here playing opposite Greer Garson, was the most popular leading man in American films in the thirties.

80 million in 1932 and 1933. By the summer of 1933 one-third of all theaters had closed. As the decade went on, however, the industry slowly found its feet; and despite continuing economic crises in other areas, the 1930s proved a key period for American cinema.

Society during the Depression provided a ready audience for escapist or glamorous movies. A number of new film genres emerged, and with them came some of the screen's best-loved actors and actresses. Two technological innovations—the introduction of sound and the advent of color movies (see box, page 97)—revolutionized the industry. By the end of the decade Hollywood had become the world's largest and most powerful producer and distributor of films.

1. THE END OF THE SILENT ERA

Hollywood's growth at the end of the twenties was primarily related to the dawn of the "talkies." Sound had been used in films for the first time in 1926—in the feature film *Don Juan*, complete with sound effects and music, but no dialogue—and this led to a boom in film production and box office sales. The silent era ended in 1927 with the release of *The Jazz Singer*, starring Al Jolson. The film featured a number of songs, and at the end of one of them Jolson turned to the camera and announced prophetically: "Wait a minute…. You ain't heard nothing yet!" Audiences were delighted to see fictional characters talking to the camera and flocked to the theaters to hear their favorite stars of the silent era speak and sing. As a result, total U.S. cinema attendance increased from 57 million in 1927 to 110 million in 1930.

Sound encouraged the growth of new genres such as musicals and gangster pictures. It also altered existing forms such as comedy and horror. A completely new style of acting was developed. In silent movies, exaggerated expressions and gestures were used to convey emotions. Now that their voices

could be heard, actors were able to give much more subtle and realistic performances.

The boundaries of film were also pushed back in an attempt to compete with the radio, which underwent a boom in the thirties and was considered a real threat by movie studios. Radio enjoyed success with dance music and comedy shows, two styles that also continually filled theaters.

2. FINDING WORK IN HOLLYWOOD

Some stars moved from radio into film. Hollywood also attracted talent from literature. William Faulkner and F. Scott Fitzgerald were among other authors who

moved to Los Angeles—sometimes reluctantly—to work as scriptwriters.

During the Depression theater also underwent a crisis. Because it was traditionally a more expensive entertainment than the cinema, audiences stayed away. Broadway directors like Preston Sturges

Greta Garbo and Lionel Barrymore in a scene from George Cukor's Camille, *1937.*

(1898–1959) and George Cukor (1899–1983) moved to Hollywood. Many theatrical actors, including James Cagney and Spencer Tracy, made the journey west as well. Thousands of theater extras, including musicians and stage mechanics, also found work in the film industry.

The United States, and Hollywood in particular, attracted many important figures from European cinema in the thirties. Stars like the Swedish Greta Garbo and Swiss-born Emil Jannings (1884–1950), as well as the French director Jean

Renoir (1894–1979) and Fritz Lang (1894–1979) from Austria, moved to America to escape instabilities in their own countries following World War I.

The development of sound was expensive. Studios had to invest in new equipment and were forced to find financial backing. In the early thirties most studios had to lay off workers and force those they kept to work longer hours for less pay. As a result, many unions and guilds, such as the Screen Actors Guild and the Writers Guild, originated in this era.

3. THE THEATERS

Between 1930 and 1933 many theaters struggled financially. They were forced to lower their admission fees and offer a number of incentives to their audiences.

Children lining up for an Easter Sunday matinee movie in the Black Belt, Chicago, Illinois.

This movie theater in Eldorado, Illinois, is charging only five cents for admission, indicating a poor population.

Many opened concession stands. To promote customer loyalty, some theaters held promotional nights. For example, on Dish Night audiences would receive different pieces of a china place setting every week until they had the complete set.

Film serials were important to ensure regular attendance. Many films would end with a cliff-hanger so that customers would come back the following week. Serials were a regular fixture at Saturday matinee shows, which were always popular with child audiences.

Newsreels were also developed during the period, and in 1935 the successful *March of Time* series of documentary films on current events was introduced.

"B" MOVIES

The need to boost ticket sales led to the birth of the double feature. "B" movies were low-cost movies, some 50 to 70 minutes in length, made to support the main feature. Usually westerns or action films, most were made by small com-

Leo the lion in a recording session for Metro-Goldwyn-Mayer's trademark.

panies known collectively as "The B-Hive" or "Poverty Row." Republic and Monogram were the most successful, producing more than 40 features a year. By 1936 double features were playing in 75 percent of all America's theaters, and sales were increasing.

"B" movies provided opportunities for young, aspiring directors and actors. Jacques Tourneur, a notable French film noir director, started out directing "B" movies for MGM. Since studios relied mainly on the appeal of the "A" movie for their profits, these supporting features were often idiosyncratic and experimental. Many have since been rediscovered and are now revered.

FILMS TO INSPIRE CONFIDENCE

In a time of crisis films started to concentrate on traditionally American preoccupations. For the first time, it seemed that hard work and perseverance did not always lead to success. Many movies of the period consequently attempted to boost Americans' self-belief by depicting individuals achieving success through their own determined, honest efforts. Other films used a "wholesome," all-American tone to boost audiences' faith in their country. Many of these films exude the confidence in the traditional American way that many individuals had come to lack.

Movie Palaces

Movie theaters gained significance during the thirties. Like many of the films they screened, they provided a glamorous counterpoint to the harsh realities of the Depression. Their fantastic architecture often conjured up images of exotic places. Several theaters' ceilings were painted with clouds and had bright lights projected onto them to give the impression that audiences were sitting outside. A trip to the movies was a kind of escapism, offering people the opportunity to forget their troubles.

4. THE STUDIO SYSTEM

Film production during the 1930s centered on seven leading Hollywood studios. Known as the "majors," these studios were Metro-Goldwyn-Mayer, Paramount, Warner Brothers, Universal, 20th Century Fox, RKO, and Columbia. Major studios owned their own theater chains and took in the majority of ticket sales profit. To keep their theaters filled, studios had to judge carefully the sorts of films the public wanted and produce the correct quantity of them.

Most studios—apart from Warners, which was very prolific—produced almost one film a week, of which about half were "B" movies. Only after they had granted their own theaters "first run" of their releases did the studios allow smaller, independent theaters to show them. Different studios were associated with particular genres and stars, and each had its defining characteristics.

METRO-GOLDWYN-MAYER

The largest studio with the most capital, Metro-Goldwyn-Mayer (MGM) catered primarily to middle-class audiences. It produced mainstream comedies and musicals, and rarely took risks with its output, preferring to avoid controversy. However, the studio reliably provided Depression-era audiences with the one thing they most wanted to see: glamor.

The studio produced polished classics starring such leading ladies as Joan Crawford, Jean Harlow (1911–1937), and Greta Garbo. MGM's major male star, Clark Gable, stayed with the studio from 1931 to 1954. The studio relied heavily on its major stars and reflected this in its promotional slogan: "More stars than there are in heaven." The loyalty of its stars

President of Warner Brothers, Harry Warner, with his wife, arriving from Hollywood in New York City, 1938. They were in the city to discuss plans to relocate their studio headquarters from New York to California.

was an important asset. Garbo, who unusually for the time never made a movie for another American studio, was constantly offered good roles and the opportunity to work with the leading production teams. A number of leading directors worked for MGM, including Cecil B. DeMille (1881–1959), one of the company's founding members.

PARAMOUNT

The second largest studio, Paramount's heyday came in the late 1930s, when it produced a number of successful light comedy dramas. Paramount made movies for the upper classes and had a more sophisticated European style and approach than the all-American MGM. Many of its stars and directors came from Germany, including Marlene Dietrich and Josef von Sternberg (1894–1969), who made a successful team. Their films together include *Morocco* (1930),

Dietrich's first American film, and *Shanghai Express* (1932). The studio was declared bankrupt in 1933, but was reorganized and found its feet again in 1935.

WARNER BROTHERS

Warner Brothers was the third most important studio in the 1930s. Warners sparked the sound revolution with *The Jazz Singer* and made the first full-length, all-talking film, *Lights of New York* (1928). Its pioneering achievements brought huge financial rewards. Throughout the thirties the studio was prolific, churning out roughly 100 pictures a year.

Warners' most notable director was the Hungarian Michael Curtiz, who made a number of key movies in different genres. Errol Flynn starred in several action-adventure pictures for the studio.

UNIVERSAL

One of the most successful studios in the silent era, Universal suffered from the arrival of sound. However, it did produce some critically acclaimed films, including the Academy Award-winning *All Quiet on the Western Front* (1930). It was one of the few successful war films of the thirties, partly because it reflected antiwar sentiments popular in the United States. The studio remains best known for its low-budget horror films, such as *Frankenstein* and *Dracula*, both directed in 1931 by James Whale (1896–1957).

Overexpenditure led to Universal's near-bankruptcy in 1935. It was saved primarily by the success of Deanna Durbin in a number of lightweight musicals.

20TH CENTURY FOX

In 1935 two studios merged to form 20th Century Fox, which never reached the status of the big three, despite using directors like John Ford (1895–1973) and Fritz Lang toward the end of the decade. It had some success with the Charlie Chan detective series, but had to work within a tighter budget than the big three.

RKO

Formed with the specific purpose of taking advantage of sound, RKO made a variety of hit-and-miss pictures in the thirties. All too often it relied on the appeal of its contract stars, among whom were Fred Astaire, Ginger Rogers, Katharine Hepburn, and Cary Grant. Hepburn and Grant starred in the screwball comedy *Bringing Up Baby* (1938). Other gems included John Ford's *The Informer* (1935) and *King Kong* (1933). This last movie, the story of a giant ape terrorizing New York, used innovative effects and earned the studio almost $2 million.

Motion picture poster for King Kong, *RKO's most profitable movie, starring Fay Wray, Robert Armstrong, and Bruce Cabot.*

COLUMBIA

The poorest of the major studios, Columbia would have gone broke had it not been for its key asset,

---

Working-class Films

Most of Warners' output was made for, and concerned, the working classes. More than any other studio, Warners focused on the contemporary world and evoked the Depression in both the content and look of its films. Its social dramas showed indictments of the penal system (*I Am a Fugitive from a Chain Gang*, 1932) and racism (*They Won't Forget*, 1937). Warners often probed underworld characters, especially in its successful gangster cycles. Even its musicals were hard-edged, concerning industrious people struggling to get to the top.

Movie Stars of the 1930s

The thirties featured many of the most famous movie stars, many of whom were first or second generation Americans whom audiences could see had made the American dream come true. Among the stars of the thirties were:

Fred Astaire (1899–1987)
Lionel Barrymore (1878–1954)
Humphrey Bogart (1899–1957)
James Cagney (1899–1986)
Charlie Chaplin (1889–1987)
Gary Cooper (1901–1961)
Joan Crawford (1908–1977)
Bette Davis (1908–1989)
Marlene Dietrich (1901–1992)
W. C. Fields (1880–1946)
Errol Flynn (1909–1959)
Clark Gable (1901–1960)
Greta Garbo (1905–1990)
Judy Garland (1922–1969)
Cary Grant (1904–1986)
Jean Harlow (1911–1937)
Katharine Hepburn (1907–)
Boris Karloff (1887–1969)
Vivien Leigh (1913–1967)
Bela Lugosi (1882–1956)
Groucho Marx (1895–1977)
Paul Muni (1895–1967)
Edward G. Robinson (1893–1973)
Ginger Rogers (1911–1995)
Shirley Temple (1928–)
Spencer Tracy (1900–1967)
John Wayne (1907–1979)
Mae West (1892–1980)

Italian-born director Frank Capra (1897–1991). Capra was hired in the late 1920s by Harry Cohn, Columbia's longtime president.

The studio's main successes were Capra's comedies, including *It Happened One Night* (1934) and *You Can't Take It with You* (1938), and Howard Hawks's (1896–1977) screwball comedies starring Cary Grant, such as *The Awful Truth* and *Holiday*. With relatively

Promotional motion picture poster for Bordertown, *featuring Paul Muni and Bette Davis.*

little money to keep stars under contract itself, Columbia often used stars and directors it "borrowed" from other studios.

STUDIO MOVIE STARS

Movie stars were an extremely influential aspect of the studio system. Studios relied on their stars to provide glamor and romance, and many received lucrative contract deals based primarily on their appearance, and not their acting skills. Studios did all they could to build and maintain audience loyalty to their stars through advertising. Promotional material for films often focused on the star as opposed to the director or plot.

During the Depression film stars took on a kind of hero status among the public. At the same time, however, like directors, they lost much of their independence. Pay packets became smaller, and many stars found themselves tied by contract to appear in films for just one studio. A refusal to take the roles offered to them could lead to serious consequences.

From time to time, studios would "lend" their stars to each other. MGM loaned Clark Gable to Columbia for *It Happened One Night*, since none of Columbia's stars were interested in the movie. Columbia, in return, let the film's director, Frank Capra, make a picture for MGM. However, intense rivalry existed between the studios over their stars, who were the source of great publicity. One example is the publicity war between Paramount and MGM, which both claimed to have the number-one imported actress—Paramount had Marlene Dietrich, and MGM had Greta Garbo.

Criticism of the Studios

The studio system has been criticized for its factorylike methods of production. Studios often crushed individualism, and many talented and original artists felt restrained. Every element of film production, from screenwriting to shooting to editing, was carried out on a regular, cost-effective basis.

Busby Berkeley inspecting girls for the chorus of a forthcoming movie in Hollywood in 1934.

the release of *The Jazz Singer* in 1927 songs and musical interludes were included in many pictures. Many film versions of stage musicals and operas were released.

In the early days of sound the major studios produced cinematic revues—films made up of a collection of star turns and set pieces. MGM released a highly successful series of "Broadway Melodies" based on this format. Many early musicals were produced quickly to capitalize on the novelty of sound.

Before long, original musicals were being written for the screen by composers such as Irving Berlin (1888-1989) and Cole Porter (1893–1964). One of the key figures in thirties musicals was choreographer Busby Berkeley (1895–1976).

Gold Diggers

Berkeley's choreography is best seen in director Mervyn LeRoy's musical *Gold Diggers of 1933*. This

5. FILM GENRES

Several new film genres evolved in the thirties. Each conformed to strict rules of narrative and form, and was carefully calculated to ensure box-office success. These genres, described below, included musicals, comedies, gangster movies, dramas, and horror films.

MUSICALS

There had previously been some "silent musicals," with specially written scores sent out to theater orchestras, but 1930s musicals were self-sufficient packages. After

Fred Astaire and Ginger Rogers were a popular song-and-dance team during the Depression.

film follows three chorus girls (Trixie, Carol, and Polly) looking for work in the Depression. They are visited by a producer, Barney, who is preparing a new show but lacks funding. At the girls' apartment he overhears their neighbor, Brad, playing the piano and discovers that he is a talented singer-songwriter able to put up the money for the show. The show goes into production, and Brad and Polly soon become engaged. However, Brad's brother and a lawyer suddenly appear and disapprove of the marriage, claiming the relationship is unequal. (Brad is from a wealthy Boston family, whereas Polly is a mere showgirl.) The two men soon fall in love with Trixie and Carol, however, and the film ends happily with a series of engage-ments and marriages.

Although *Gold Diggers* was primarily supposed to entertain, it also offered an early example of the sort of social awareness that became typical of LeRoy's later work. The film opens with a ren-dition of "We're in the Money,"

Busby Berkeley

Berkeley worked on Broadway as a dance director before joining MGM, where he contributed significantly to the development of the musical. He tried out new cinematic techniques, such as rhythmical cutting (editing the production numbers to fit the rhythms of the music) and striking kaleidoscopic effects. To achieve the latter, he attached the camera to swooping cranes to shoot scores of dancing girls from a number of different angles. His "top shots," as they were called, highlighted the complex, geometric patterns made by the dancers—patterns closely related to the formalism of contemporary Art Deco design.

sung by showgirls in costumes made from gold coins. This routine is interrupted by the police, and the show's costumes and props are confiscated due to unpaid debts. The repossession of goods shows that LeRoy is at least partly concerned with depicting the economic reality of the period. The plot is also of social importance, with the marriages at the end representing a leveling of the social classes, bringing together aristo-crats, businessmen, and showgirls.

Most of the early Hollywood musicals were simply filmed versions of theater productions, usually shown from one angle, just as the audience would see it on stage. Berkeley's unusual camera angles and deft editing between camera angles made *Gold Diggers* instantly more cinematic than theatrical. The film is also a good example of the popular "backstage musical" genre, where the main characters in a movie are themselves working on a musical within the film.

Song-and-Dance Teams
Films featuring song-and-dance teams came to replace Berkeley's opulent routines in the thirties. RKO relied on its lucrative series of musicals starring Fred Astaire and Ginger Rogers, who appeared in 10 films together. Like Berk-eley, Astaire came to movies from Broadway and found instant success in film musicals. His pictures with Ginger Rogers were elegant and sophisticated, and more graceful than Berkeley's

Comedian W. C. Fields dressed as a bank guard in The Bank Dick *(1940), one of 25 talking pictures he starred in from 1930.*

Child Stars

Children made regular appearances in musicals. Deanna Durbin (1921–) starred in a number of productions, as did Mickey Rooney. Rooney often acted opposite Judy Garland, the greatest female musical star, most memorably in *Babes in Arms* (1939). Shirley Temple enjoyed a string of commercially successful pictures. One of her most famous moments came in *Bright Eyes* (1934), when she sang the catchy song "On the Good Ship Lollipop." President Roosevelt summed up the child star's appeal in 1935: "During this Depression, when the spirit of the people is lower than at any other time, it is a splendid thing that for just 15 cents, an American can go to a movie, look at the smiling face of a baby and forget his troubles."

Child star Shirley Temple (right) in the children's classic Heidi *(1937), based on a book by Swiss author Johanna Spyri.*

flamboyant productions. The team behind their pictures boasted top-quality composers and directors. Fred and Ginger's best films, *Top Hat* (1935)—with songs by Irving Berlin—and *Shall We Dance* (1937)—with a score by George and Ira Gershwin—were directed by Mark Sandrich. Their dance routines were meticulously planned and rehearsed, and Astaire made sure that they were integral to the plot. The gradual unification of plot and music was a key development of the musical in the period.

COMEDY
The comic film underwent a huge transformation in the Depression. The sound era called for a completely different kind of comic

acting. Visual gags and clowning were replaced by witty dialogue and verbal confusion. Comedy no longer relied on individual comedians, and more collaborative efforts were developed. Styles that had proved popular in the theater soon found their way onto the big screen. In the early thirties there were a number of successful chaotic farces that relied on far-fetched misunderstandings and outrageous coincidences for humorous effect. A type of farce called the comedy of errors proved popular. In this sort of film characters typically became involved in ludicrous cases of mistaken identity. Another type of comedy, the so-called comedy of manners, played on the gap between rich and poor.

Comedy and Sound
The three great comedians of the silent era—Charlie Chaplin, Buster Keaton (1895–1966), and Harold Lloyd (1894-1971)—dealt with the arrival of sound in different ways. Chaplin used soundtracks and sound effects, but no dialogue. Lloyd's voice proved unsuitable for his comic style, and his talkies were largely unpopular. Keaton, who had been MGM's highest-paid comedian at the end of the 1920s, made several averagely successful slapstick features, but never really settled into sound.

Many New York stage comics crossed over into cinema as wise-crack comedy became popular. W. C. Fields and Mae West delivered wisecrack gags that they wrote themselves. Fields created the persona of a pompous, overbearing fraud with a dislike of children. A constant moaner, his nagging wife was often the cause for his grief. As well as writing his own scripts, and improvising much of the action as he went along, Fields also directed a number of his own films. Mae West's routines tended to rely more on her seductive image and on sexual innuendo and double entendres. At the time of the Production Code (see box, page 94), such performances were sometimes condemned as threatening to American decency. West also formed a successful comic partnership with Cary Grant in films *She Done Him Wrong* (1933) and *I'm No Angel* (1933).

Comic Partnerships

A specially crazy kind of comedy was developed by the Marx Brothers, who moved into film careers straight from vaudeville. The five brothers and their mother originally performed as "The Six Musical Mascots" and achieved considerable success on the stage. Despite this success, one of the brothers—Gummo— left the act. The four remaining

brothers continued to write and perform their own material and appeared on Broadway. Their first movies were adaptations of their

Comedian Groucho Marx often appeared on stage with an oversized cigar and a ludicrous painted moustache.

plays. These anarchic pictures, such as *The Cocoanuts* (1929) and *Animal Crackers* (1930), blended both silent and sound cinematic techniques. The humor relied on the interplay between the brothers, each of whom had his own distinctive appearance and character. The wisecracking Groucho, with his huge cigar and ludicrously painted moustache, was the best known. The Marx Brothers made a few highly inventive, fast-paced movies for Paramount, the best of which was the imaginative *Duck Soup* (1933).

Laurel and Hardy

Like the Marx Brothers, Stan Laurel (1890–1965) and Oliver Hardy (1892–1957) learned their comic trade performing in vaudeville. Both had also acted in silent films before they teamed up in 1926 at the suggestion of studio boss Hal Roach, whom both had approached for work. *Putting Pants on Philip* (1927), their first feature film, used dialogue sparingly and mainly for plot development, like many of the first talkies. The pair's humor relied on visual and verbal contrasts—the skinny, nervy Laurel was the counterpoint to the overweight, pompous Hardy. Together the unlikely pair bumbled their way from catastrophe to catastrophe in almost 90 movies.

Charlie Chaplin

Charlie Chaplin was born into a poor family in London. Following his mother and brother, he started in vaudeville at a young age. While appearing on stage in America, Chaplin was given the opportunity to star in a film. In his second feature he invented his own character, "the little tramp." Both comic and tragic, Chaplin played this character in a number of films. Significantly for audiences at the time, the tramp always backed the underdog and the downtrodden. His appearance—baggy trousers, bowler hat, walking stick, and oversized shoes—made him instantly recognizable worldwide. Many believe Chaplin to be the first genuine international star of cinema.

Chaplin directed many of his own films and was famously opposed to the arrival of sound. *Modern Times* (1936) is widely acknowledged to be the last of the great silent movies. The film follows a series of events experienced by the little tramp, who appears for the last time in the film. During the picture the tramp tries to deal with a factory assembly line, falls in love, and is arrested when he finds himself in the middle of a union demonstration. He takes cocaine in jail and on his release tries and fails to hold down different jobs.

The tramp experiences many universal emotions, such as love and fear, and so his adventures proved instantly popular with people all over the world. Chaplin frequently drew on his own experiences to add an extra element of realism to his pictures. He injected much social comment within the humor, and in this way his films are similar to some of Busby Berkeley's musicals. *Modern Times* in particular graphically highlights the poverty of the Great Depression.

Charlie Chaplin performing before a large crowd with a megaphone, 1935.

Screwball Comedy

Screwball comedies, made for only a relatively short time, were very popular in the Depression. These sophisticated movies grew out of the wisecracking comedy practiced by performers like Mae West. They usually featured social and sexual role inversion and extremes of class and milieu.

In the typical screwball film an overly serious male had his world turned upside down by his relationship with an uninhibited female. The comedy relied on the interplay between these two contrasting characters.

Often the woman seemed to be in control in screwball. This appealed to female audiences, who found comedies a welcome diversion from the harsh realities of Depression-era life.

Frank Capra directed the first of the screwball comedies, *It Happened One Night*. This wayward adventure follows the growing love affair between two characters played by Claudette Colbert (1903–1996) and Clark Gable. It was the first film to be awarded all five major Academy Awards (for Best Picture, Actor, Actress, Screenplay, and Director.) The film's message was designed to go down well with Depression-era audiences. Colbert's character has everything yet is unhappy, whereas Gable has nothing but manages to find happiness through simple pleasures. Colbert is slowly converted to Gable's way of thinking. Female viewers were supposed to leave with the impression that rich girls would be happier in the position of married working-class women, who might be poor but still had love. *It Happened One Night* opened up the way for other screwball directors such as Preston Sturges and Howard Hawks.

Capra is famous for making romantic comedies with everyday small-town folk. Examples include *Mr. Deeds Goes to Town* (1936) and *It's a Wonderful Life* (1946). He provided audiences with reassuring pictures that showed simple American virtues triumphing over adversity in the final reckoning, encouraging them to not worry. His Robert Riskin-scripted comedies were of great social importance, and Capra made most of his best films in the thirties. He was later criticized for the very patriotic, oversentimental style that made him so popular at the time. Some critics dubbed his style "Capracorn"; today his reputation is once again high.

GANGSTER FILMS

The striking aura associated with gangster films was first developed in the 1930s. The earliest crime pictures are saturated with mean hoodlums, glamorous molls, guns, alcohol, and sharp suits. Most of the action takes place at night, against a hostile backdrop of rainy, neon-lit streets.

Powerful silent movies had been made within the genre previously, such as Josef von Sternberg's classic *Underworld* (1927). These films would often have been accompanied by sound from the theater's orchestra. However, the arrival of sound in films added an extra dimension to

gangster movies, bringing action to life in a more realistic and thus more thrilling way.

Between 1930 and 1932 roughly 60 gangster films were made in Hollywood. The talkies made crime seem much more glamorous than it had been in the silents. The gangster cycle started with *Little Caesar* (1930), followed by *The Public Enemy* (1931) and *Scarface* (1932). These movies offered a different escapism from musicals and comedies. Based on fact, most took their inspiration from crime reports in newspapers. Crime was rife in the Depression,

The prototype of the stuffy male character in screwball was Cary Grant, seen here with costar Katharine Hepburn in a scene from Howard Hawks' film Bringing Up Baby.

with so many dissatisfied citizens forced through hunger and desperation to commit acts of bank robbery, theft, and prostitution, not to mention illegal drinking and gang warfare (see Volume 3, Chapter 5, "Crime in the Depression"). Several onscreen gangsters were based on real-life criminals, such as Al Capone.

Little Caesar

The first great gangster movie of the sound era, Mervyn LeRoy's *Little Caesar,* instantly gave rise to a number of imitations. Adapted by William Riley Burnett from his novel of the same name, the screenplay is written in a style similar to the novel: terse, understated, and precise. It contains many notable one-liners, from the announcement of Rico, a small-time crook who rises to become a big shot in Chicago: "All right you guys—I'm boss here—see?" to his dying words: "Mother of God…is this the end of Rico?"

The film starred Edward G. Robinson as Rico. Born in Bucharest, Romania, Robinson moved to New York when he was 10 years old. He appeared in many crime and detective films. Remembered as mild and gentle in his private life, he repeatedly gave convincing cinematic portrayals of man's capacity for violence.

The Public Enemy

Actor James Cagney achieved instant recognition in 1931 with Warner Brothers' *The Public Enemy* and remained virtually inseparable from the studio for the rest of his career. He proved to be the most influential actor within the gangster movie genre, and his unscrupulous and explosive gangster stereotype has been copied by many actors since.

The Public Enemy depicts the downward spiral of a criminal thought to be based on "Little Hymie" Weiss, the leader of the North Side Chicago Gang. A fast-moving, violent film, it shows crime to be primarily the product of poverty and poor social conditions. Originally cast in a supporting role, Cagney was so impressive during rehearsals that he was given the lead. The film is

The gangster actor as family man: Edward G. Robinson (center) greets an acquaintance while traveling with his family.

Gangster Heroes

The key actors in the gangster genre—James Cagney, Edward G. Robinson, Humphrey Bogart, and even Clark Gable—were popular heroes at a time when ordinary Americans, disillusioned with politicians, bankers, and businessmen, needed heroes more than ever. The stars seemed to be untouched by economic plight. The gangsters they played were also seen as heroes, taking matters into their own hands and achieving success through individual endeavor.

Scarface

The release of Howard Hawks's *Scarface—Shame of a Nation* was delayed for many months due to a long censorship dispute that led to many of the film's scenes being cut. *Scarface* was the first gangster film to actually show a criminal using a machine gun. It contains what was at the time a staggering death toll of 28. The film, which gained instant notoriety on its release, has been surrounded by legends ever since. One story ran that the film's producers unsuccessfully offered Al Capone himself $200,000 to appear in the film, which in many aspects resembled the story of his own rise to power in Chicago.

Scarface focuses on the Chicago gang wars and the battle for power between two gangsters: Tony Camonte (played by Paul Muni) and Gaffney (Boris Karloff). It also features the romance between Camonte's sister

famous for a number of classic moments, including the breakfast table scene, where a furious Cagney mashes a grapefruit into Mae Clarke's face.

The Hays Office

In 1922, following a significant number of scandals involving Hollywood personalities, the people responsible for the film industry formed the Motion Picture Producers and Distributors of America (MPPDA). It was a self-regulating body set up to fend off the threat of government censorship of films and to create a positive image of the film industry. Will H. Hays (1879–1954), a national politician, was made president of the association, a position he held until 1945. A highly respected figure, Hays organized the drawing up of a moral blacklist in Hollywood and added moral clauses to authors' contracts.

As for the films themselves, the frank approach of some of Hollywood's creations—for example, realistic violence in the gangster movies and over-explicit sexual scenes in some of the early Mae West films—did not impress certain censorship groups, although it would be considered tame today. In 1930, therefore, Hays and several others issued the Production Code, a detailed account of what was considered morally acceptable on screen. Drug addiction, alcoholism, bad language, blasphemy, and nudity were all banned. The code effectively put an end to the gritty realism of the early talkies. It helped box office sales, however, by ensuring regular family audiences.

The strength of Hays' personal influence on the censorship office of the MPPDA was such that it became known as the Hays Office.

Dinner club scene from Howard Hawks' film Scarface, *showing actors Paul Muni and Osgood Perkins competing to light a cigarette for actress Karen Morley.*

and his henchman. Camonte has strong feelings for his sister and is driven to murder his henchman, believing he has violated her. The film had a sardonic element that was rare for the genre at this time.

Censorship of Movies

The gangster movies released at the start of the decade are unique in that the action is seen from the criminal's viewpoint. Although the good guys would always triumph at the end of the movie, somehow the lasting impression for the audience was of the dynamic nature of the criminals. They were shown to be in complete control and were always one step ahead of the police. Such depictions were banned by the Hays Office, which believed they glorified gangsters' violent lives.

Until the ban was lifted years later, gangster movies throughout the rest of the decade were told from the point of view of the police officers fighting to uphold justice. Toward the end of the 1930s the FBI's "G-Men" were in power, both on the streets and on the screen. Led by J. Edgar Hoover, the director of the FBI, this dedicated team of crime-fighters did their best to stamp out the sort of crimes Americans had enjoyed watching in movies for years.

HORROR FILMS

A number of seminal horror films were released during the thirties. Many of them were heavily influenced by their silent forerunners

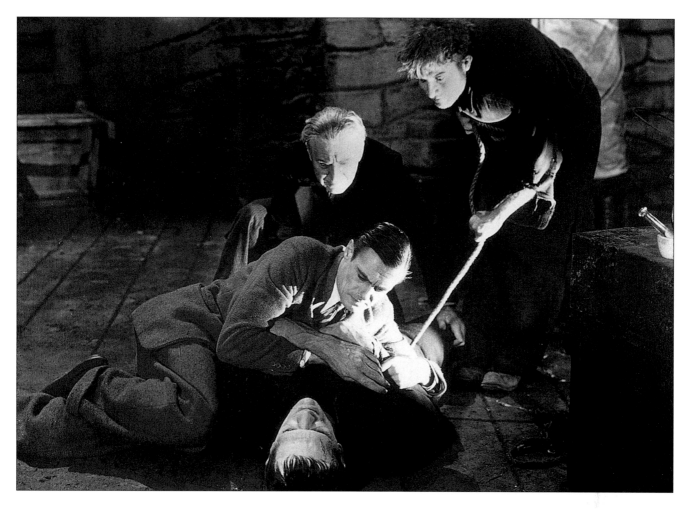

Dr. Frankenstein wrestles with the monster in this scene from the horror movie Frankenstein.

and had a Germanic tinge, using stylized sets to add a ghostly atmosphere. Many were adapted from stories written by horror and mystery writers like Edgar Allan Poe (1809–1849). The best horror movies were made by Universal, which had two great directors in Tod Browning and James Whale. Tod Browning's 1931 version of the Bram Stoker novel *Dracula* was well received by audiences and critics, and is said to be the definitive sound adaptation of the novel. The film features an intense performance by the Hungarian actor Bela Lugosi, who had played the part on Broadway four years earlier. *Dracula* became the proto-type of numerous later Hollywood vampire films.

At the end of 1931 Universal had another horror smash hit with Whale's *Frankenstein*. Lugosi turned down the offer of the Monster role, paving the way for Boris Karloff, who reappeared in Universal's *The Mummy* in 1932. Universal also set the trend for horror sequels. Frankenstein was followed in 1935 by the equally successful *Bride of Frankenstein*. Having witnessed the success of Universal's horror pictures, many other studios experimented with the genre.

FILM DRAMA

A number of social dramas attempted to depict the struggles of ordinary working people during the Depression. *A Man's Castle* (1933) starred Spencer Tracy and Loretta Young struggling to make ends meet in a dilapidated New York shack. King Vidor's *Our Daily Bread* (1934) told of the problems encountered by an agricultural cooperative during the Depression. This new breed of realist films had much in common with some of the literature of the period, such as the novels of James T. Farrell and John Steinbeck, whose *Grapes of Wrath* (1939) was later adapted for the big screen. Although gritty and powerful, films depicting misery and homelessness inevitably failed at the box office, as audiences opted for the more light-hearted musicals and comedies.

Depression-themed dramas were satirized by Preston Sturges in *Sullivan's Travels* (1941). Sturges

Walt Disney and Animation

American animator and producer Walt Disney (1901–1966, below) achieved much success in the Depression, receiving the Academy Award for cartoons every year in the 1930s. The popularity of his early features, *Steamboat Willie* (1928) and *The Three Little Pigs* (1933), inspired him to think about creating a much longer cartoon, which would be roughly the same length as a real feature film. The result, *Snow White and the Seven Dwarfs* (1937), took four years to make and cost $1.5 million. Disney took a huge risk with the picture, artistically and financially. Before it was released, *Snow White* was nicknamed "Disney's Folly" by people in Hollywood because few believed it would succeed. However, it proved to be a great box-office hit. The film's popularity even helped the struggling U.S. toy industry with a number of linked marketing products. Disney also produced numerous shorter movies during the decade, including *The Three Little Pigs*. The pigs' cheerfully defiant song "Who's Afraid of the Big Bad Wolf" particularly appealed to an audience seeking reasons for optimism.

pokes fun at well-meaning directors in this tale of a director (Sullivan) who decides to live with down-and-outs in order to study society. While researching his over-earnest picture, tentatively titled "Brother, Where Art Thou?" Sullivan realizes that what audiences really need are movies to make them laugh and distract them from their worries. Similar conclusions were reached by real-life directors.

6. THE FILM INDUSTRY RECOVERS

By the end of the decade Hollywood had fully recovered from the Depression, with 1939 widely regarded as one of the most productive years in American cinema.

John Ford's influential masterpiece *Stagecoach* was released and is often hailed as the first modern western. It was filmed in Monument Valley, Arizona, where Ford made eight more films. The same year brought *The Roaring Twenties*, a gangster movie starring Humphrey Bogart and James Cagney. A pseudo-documentary with a retrospective feel, the picture evoked the Depression by focusing on unemployment and corruption.

It was a good year for musicals too. A 16-year-old Judy Garland starred in the much-loved *Wizard*

Introduction of Color

The coming of sound in the movies temporarily affected another great technological innovation of the era, color pictures. By the early 1920s most features included at least one sequence in color, produced by tinting black-and-white film. When it became clear that such tinting interfered with the transmission of sound, the practice stopped.

In 1928 the Technicolor Corporation developed a new two-color production process to mass produce high-quality prints that could be screened on normal projectors. In 1932 Technicolor made color more realistic by introducing a system that used all three primary colors.

Technicolor's system dominated the industry for around 25 years and gave the corporation great power, since it rented all the equipment and staff to production companies. There were other drawbacks: The cameras were too bulky for easy location filming, for example. As a result, color caught on only slowly in the thirties. Walt Disney used it for *Snow White* (1937). It was also used in *The Adventures of Robin Hood* (1938), *The Wizard of Oz* (1939), and *Gone with the Wind* (1939). For studios and filmgoers alike, color remained closely associated with glamor, fantasy, and spectacle.

American movie actor John Wayne in a scene from his classic western Stagecoach.

of Oz, which featured a superb score, stunning Technicolor sequences, and elaborate makeup and costumes. The decade's vogue for costume drama based on historical figures and events climaxed with the four-hour period epic *Gone with the Wind*. Set during the Civil War, it starred Vivien Leigh as Scarlett O'Hara opposite Clark Gable as Rhett Butler. As the country itself prepared for World War II, 1939 rounded off a remarkably fertile decade of American cinema.

CHRONICLERS OF THE GREAT DEPRESSION

Momentous periods in history have always produced chroniclers who try to capture the spirit of the era. During the Depression many writers and journalists, photographers and musicians recorded the experiences of ordinary people living at that time, both in fiction and nonfiction. Today their works provide a valuable insight into what life was like in America in the 1930s.

Just as writers like F. Scott Fitzgerald (1896–1940) helped define the spirit of the 1920s Jazz Age in novels such as *The Great Gatsby* (1925), so writers in the 1930s were important in characterizing the spirit of their age. Many writers believed it was important to chronicle the experience of the crisis. The result was that the decade was one of the most self-reflective of any in American culture.

Writing had many functions in the 1930s. In newspapers and magazines it was often a form of protest and propaganda, both for and against government policy and political philosophies such as communism and capitalism. Photojournalism, which combined

A newsboy sells newspapers on a street in New York City. People continued buying newspapers throughout the Depression, since they wanted to keep informed about economic and other matters, both in their own country and abroad.

The American Dream

The American Dream dates back to the arrival of the first settlers in America. For them America was a land of hope and a refuge from religious repression and persecution that held the promise of material and spiritual happiness. The same remained true for many generations of immigrants who found freedom and fortune in the United States. During the Depression, when for many migrants California became the new embodiment of the Promised Land, many writers questioned whether the "dream" that had endured throughout much of the nation's history still, or ever had, existed.

writing with images, provided visual evidence of the hardships people suffered. Literature reflected the Depression by depicting characters experiencing hardships like those of contemporary readers. Meanwhile, popular fiction allowed readers to escape into worlds of adventure and romance far removed from the realities of daily life. Many magazines offered escapism through short stories or reflected the Depression in lifestyle articles.

1. LITERARY WRITING

Literary authors who wrote during the Depression can be divided into two main groups—those who wrote about the Depression, and those who chose to write about subjects not directly associated with it. One of the best-known novelists who wrote about the experiences of people living in the Depression was John Steinbeck (1902–1968).

JOHN STEINBECK

Steinbeck's novels were both well written and easy to read. He was dismissed by many literary critics,

Steinbeck is best known for his novel The Grapes of Wrath, *now considered an American classic.*

particularly on the East Coast, as a "popular" writer. However, the controversy his novels provoked,

especially among conservatives, suggests that his works were taken more seriously than these critics gave credit for. He was accused of being a communist revolutionary by those on the right, while left-wingers criticized him for not being revolutionary enough.

Born on February 27, 1902, in Salinas County, California, John Ernst Steinbeck enjoyed an unremarkable upbringing in a middle-class family. His parents were important to his success as a writer. Steinbeck's mother was a schoolteacher and encouraged him to read widely. Later, his father was to provide financial support during the bleak years when Steinbeck

The Federal Writers' Project

Roosevelt set up various arts projects as part of the New Deal Works Progress Administration (WPA). One of these projects, designed specifically for writers, was the Federal Writers' Project (FWP). Headed by Henry G. Alsberg, the FWP found work for jobless writers, journalists, and editors at a wage of around $20 a week. At its peak the FWP employed about 6,700 people with a broad range of writing experience. It also provided literary apprenticeships to a number of future famous writers.

The *American Guide* series remains the FWP's most famous project. This series of guidebooks, published in 1941, provided an invaluable insight into life in the United States during the Depression. The content of the books ranged from geographical information and architecture, to the cultural history of a particular region or state.

Less well known is that the FWP also recorded the life stories of more than 10,000 people from different occupations, areas, and ethnic groups, including former slaves and sharecroppers. Other products of the project were biographies, studies of racial groups, and social and local histories.

The project was operated by the WPA from 1935 to 1939, and after the Depression the project was transfered to state sponsorship.

FWP staff working on the American Guide *series. The guides explored in detail the history and everyday life of a state or region. They were filled with factual information on local customs and politics, as well as local tales.*

was trying to establish himself as a writer. Steinbeck attended Stanford University, where he studied marine biology, but left without graduating and took on a number of temporary laboring jobs. He met his wife, Carol Henning, while showing her around a fish hatchery where he was working. They moved to San Francisco and married in 1930. Steinbeck had continued to write, but his work received little attention.

Early Novels

Steinbeck's first commercial success came in 1935 with his novel *Tortilla Flat*, a sympathetic story of a group of amoral, hedonistic friends living in an upscale district in California. His next two novels, *In Dubious Battle* (1936) and *Of Mice and Men* (1937), focused on the theme of the new class of migrant worker that appeared in the Depression.

The Grapes of Wrath

The theme of the migrant worker was given its greatest emphasis in the Pulitzer Prize-winning *The Grapes of Wrath* (1939). It tells the story of the Joad family, who own a farm in the Dust Bowl region of Oklahoma. As crops fail and their farm is repossessed, they are forced to head west to the "promised land" of California in search of a new life (see Volume 3, Chapter 4, "California in the 1930s"). The novel describes the terrible living conditions endured by the Okies, both on the road and once they arrive in California, as well as their experiences of hunger and prejudice. As one character observes, "Okie use'ta mean you was from Oklahoma. Now it

A scene from the 1940 film of The Grapes of Wrath, *showing the Joad family in their truck.*

Migrant workers were the subject of several of Steinbeck's novels, including Of Mice and Men.

means you're scum." Despite hardships, desertions, and the deaths of Granma and Grampa, the Joads continue their journey ("It don't take no nerve to do somepin when there ain't nothin' else you can do"). Predictably, California fails to live up to their hopes, and they end the novel, once again, staring starvation in the face.

Steinbeck's Legacy

Steinbeck's reputation declined toward the end of his career, and this, together with false accusations of communism, made him depressed. He has been accused

James T. Farrell, author of the Studs Lonigan trilogy, expressed anger at social injustice in his highly realistic novels.

ment that some female characters in contemporary fiction, such as Ma Joad in Steinbeck's *The Grapes of Wrath*, never articulate.

Agnes Smedley

Agnes Smedley's *Daughter of Earth* (1929) challenges the ideals of motherhood with its autobiographical story of a woman's independent search for her own vocation. Marie Rogers escapes rural poverty by first getting a teaching job and then breaking into the world of male professionals. She pays for herself to go through college and then campaigns to end British colonial rule in India. When a second edition of the novel was published in 1935, the anticolonial ending was omitted, and the suffering of

the Rogers family on their farm became the most relevant part for 1930s readers.

Meridel Le Sueur

Meridel Le Sueur's short stories of the 1930s were collected in *Salute to Spring* (1940). In many of her stories Le Sueur reinvents the traditional portrait presented in male fiction of motherhood as a supportive, harmonizing figure. Le Sueur's women are often independent, self-sufficient providers. The

Wife of a former tenant farmer with one of her five children, living on unemployment relief. Many women writers in the thirties made a conscious effort to record what life was like for women living in the Depression.

inspiration for these representations of women is likely to have come from Le Sueur's mother, who left her husband to bring up her children alone, and Le Sueur's experience of working women at the Minnesota WPA.

Tillie Olsen

Tillie Olsen wrote barely half of the manuscript for *Yonnonido* before she was interrupted by the demands of motherhood and the need to work as a domestic servant. She published parts of the novel during the 1930s in journals, but the novel as a whole did not appear until 1971.

Set in the 1930s, *Yonnondio* is a naturalistic novel that expresses disappointment with the unchanging lot of the working classes and, at the same time, celebrates the enduring nature of the human spirit. The novel focuses on the inhuman conditions of workers in a meatpacking factory in the Depression. Like Le Sueur and Smedley, Olsen had first-hand experience with the conditions endured by female factory workers, described in the novel as "hell," and the way in which they performed the jobs that "men will not take."

Josephine Herbst

Another committed leftist writer was Josephine Herbst (1892–1969). Her major work of fiction was a trilogy following the Trexler family through the early part of the 20th century. The final novel of the series, *Rope of Gold*, follows the younger members of the family through the chaos of the 1930s. Herbst drew on her journalistic experience for the novel, which examines the difficulties experienced by professional women in balancing their careers with their home lives. Herbst's central character, Victoria

Martha Gellhorn and Ernest Hemingway on a shooting expedition shortly after their marriage in 1940.

Chance, fights to become a successful reporter, but sacrifices her marriage in the process.

Martha Gellhorn

Another reporter known for her Depression fiction is Martha Gellhorn (1908–1999). Gellhorn worked as a reporter for *Collier's* during World War II and was married to writer Ernest Hemingway during that period. Her major work of fiction concerning the Depression was *The Trouble I've Seen* (1936), about workers in the city surviving on government support. As with many other Depression writings, the boundary between reportage and fiction often becomes blurred (see box, page 112).

BLACK WRITERS

An important function of the Federal Writer's Project (FWP) (see Chapter 4, "The Arts in the Depression") was that it provided literary training for many African American writers who might otherwise have been denied the opportunity. Distinguished African American writers who served apprenticeships on the FWP include: Margaret Walker (b. 1915), Ralph Ellison (1914–1994), Zora Neale Hurston (1901–1960), and Richard Wright (1908–1960).

Richard Wright

Richard Wright was born on a sharecroppers' farm in Mississippi. All of his grandparents were slaves. Wright experienced a traumatic and poor childhood. His father left home when he was five years old. Two years later his mother was paralyzed, and he was forced to live with various relatives. Wright left school at the age of 15 and educated himself. He moved first to Memphis and later to Chicago, where he became a member of the Communist Party.

Wright's *Native Son* was published in 1940 and tells of conditions in the Chicago slums. Its publication established Wright as the leading black author of the era. The novel's initial impact was remarkable: 215,000 copies of the book were sold in just three weeks. *Native Son* was the first novel by an African American to be offered as a main selection by the Book-of-

•

"…the most powerful statement we have yet of what it means to be a Negro in America."

•

the-Month Club. Such immediate popularity was surprising for an uncompromising protest novel about economic and racial injustice. Most of the black fiction of the previous decade had a more timid and sentimental tone. Wright wanted *Native Son* to be a novel that "would be so hard and deep that [readers] would have to face it without the consolation of tears."

The novel is an important social document that drew attention to many problems in contemporary America. It also influenced a new generation of black writers. James Baldwin (1924–1987), a friend of Wright, called *Native Son* "the most powerful and celebrated statement we have yet of what it means to be a Negro in America."

After *Native Son* Wright struggled to achieve the same success. He got sick, and trips to Africa worsened his condition. He died in poverty and was cremated, along with a copy of the autobiographical *Black Boy* (1945), at the Père Lachaise cemetery in Paris.

2. POPULAR FICTION

Although popular fiction may not carry the critical status of serious literature, it contains useful insights into the impulses and motivations of a culture. It also offers the modern reader the chance to examine some of the preoccupations of the period when it was written.

ESCAPIST NOVELS

People desired an escape from the realities of life. Many had plenty of time on their hands, but did not want to be reminded of their current situation. Lengthy novels set in the past provided the distant world many people sought, and the stock ingredients of romance, adventure, heroism, and sex ensured a book sold well.

Hervey Allen (1889–1949) wrote a long romantic novel set in

Richard Wright, whose powerful protest novel Native Son *won him recognition and influenced future black writers.*

Native Son

A U.S. Housing Authority on Chicago's South Side, 1933. In Native Son *Wright describes conditions in the Chicago slums.*

Native son tells the story of Bigger Thomas, an uneducated black youth living in Chicago's South Side ghetto. The novel is divided into three main sections, entitled "Fear," "Flight," and "Fate."

The first section describes Bigger's claustrophobic surroundings, his family's poverty, and the bored dissatisfaction he shares with his friends. Bigger escapes the ghetto when he is offered employment by a rich white family. He goes to work for them as a chauffeur, attracting the interests of Mary, his employer's communist daughter. On his first night Bigger drives Mary and her boyfriend out for the evening. Returning to the house with the girl, who is drunk, he helps her into bed. When the girl's blind mother is awoken and approaches the room, Bigger accidentally kills Mary, through his fear of being caught with her. When his crime is uncovered, he is forced to go on the run. The second section of the novel concerns his attempts to hide from his pursuers. During this time he also murders his girlfriend. He is caught by the police after a dramatic rooftop chase across the city.

The final part of the novel finds Bigger in his cell and also consists of his trial. Bigger develops a close friendship with his lawyer and grows to achieve a greater understanding of his life. Like the nameless black hero of Ralph Ellison's later novel *Invisible Man* (1952), Bigger learns that the oppressive white society that surrounds him offers him no identity.

Gone with the Wind

Margaret Mitchell (1900–1949) was an author and journalist from Georgia. She wrote only one novel, the Pulitzer Prize-winning *Gone with the Wind*. Financially she did not need to write another book. Published in 1936, the novel sold some 1,500,000 copies in its first year and by May 1941 had sold 3,368,000 copies in the hardback English edition. In addition, the novel was translated into 18 different languages, of which the German version was the most popular, selling 500,000 copies. *Gone with the Wind* is said to be the fastest-selling book in American publishing history: One account claims that 50,000 copies were sold in one day. The novel was also made into a phenomenally successful motion picture in 1939 from a script by Sidney Howard (1891–1939). The epic film starred glamorous Hollywood actors Clark Gable and Vivien Leigh and further enhanced the popularity of the novel.

Set in Georgia, the novel follows the adventures of Scarlett O'Hara through the Civil War and the Reconstruction period that followed. Scarlett is an independent, selfish young woman whose constant and egotistical discontentment with her lot causes her and others misery. It is only at the novel's end that she acquires some self-knowledge.

Gone with the Wind combined melodrama and romance with realistic, recognizable characters. For contemporary readers it could be interpreted either as an inspiring tale of determination in the face of adversity, or an apology for the enduring Southern system of racial segregation.

Margaret Mitchell with a copy of her best-selling novel Gone with the Wind. *Fundamentally a gripping story, it has endured the test of time.*

The wire room of the New York World Telegram and the Sun. *Newspaper circulation did not drop in the Depression.*

Napoleonic times entitled *Anthony Adverse* (1933). In two years it sold over half a million copies. Walter Edmonds (1903–) wrote historical novels about his home state of New York, including *Rome Haul* (1929), about building the Erie Canal, and *Drums along the Mohawk* (1936), which tells about the effect of the American Revolution on the farmers of the Mohawk Valley. Easily the most popular novel of the decade, however, was Margaret Mitchell's *Gone with the Wind* (see box).

3. THE PRESS

Although the circulation of local newspapers declined during the Depression, big-city papers re-mained largely unaffected by the reduction in Americans' spending power. Newspapers were not expensive, and people were still eager to know what was happening in the country and the world during the economic crisis.

Since the end of World War I in 1918 the intense battle for circulation had resulted in a trend in the press toward the consolidation of titles. The 1920s in New York saw a battle for circulation among sensational tabloid papers, including the *New York Daily News* and the *Daily Mirror*. In the 1930s takeovers led to the merger or disappearance of numerous local papers. This left fewer papers whose high circulations made them attractive to advertisers, attracting revenue that enabled them to further enhance their dominance. In a typical move of the period, for example, the

Scripps-Howard organization in 1931 bought the *New York Morning World*, *Evening World*, and *Sunday World*. It closed the morning and Sunday papers and merged the evening title with the *New York Evening Telegram*. Afternoon newspapers were particularly popular with readers during the decade.

Other innovations in the press included the development of the Teletypesetter. This machine allowed journalists in the field, and the wire services that telegraphed stories all over the country, to file stories to the newsroom that would print out on a Linotype machine already in position on the page . The rise of advertising meanwhile encouraged the use of market research to analyze readers' interests as accurately as possible. The traditional dominance of the editor in newspapers was replaced by the rise of influential columnists such

Reportage and Fiction

A significant number of Depression writers were journalists and reporters by trade. James T. Farrell, Martha Gellhorn, Tillie Olsen, Josephine Herbst, Meridel Le Sueur, Agnes Smedley, and Margaret Mitchell all reported news stories either before or during their fiction-writing careers. The crossover is partly explained by the fact that both journalism and novel writing require similar skills of observation and analysis. In a sense, writing fiction about contemporary events inevitably necessitates blending the two disciplines. Reporters have the skills to analyze and get to the roots of a story, and that is what writers of the Depression often aimed to do.

The blurring of boundaries between reportage and fiction is explicitly visible in John Dos Passos's *U.S.A.* trilogy, which weaves actual news headlines and factual biographies into his fiction. Martha Gellhorn drew on her experiences of reporting war in *The Trouble I've Seen* in order to make her work more realistic. But perhaps the best example of overlapping fiction and fact is *Let Us Now Praise Famous Men* (1941). This mainly factual work by James Agee (1909–1955), with photographs by Walker Evans (1903–1975), was originally intended as a piece of journalistic reporting about cotton tenantry. However, the pair were drawn into their subject matter and ended up expanding on their original assignment. They became

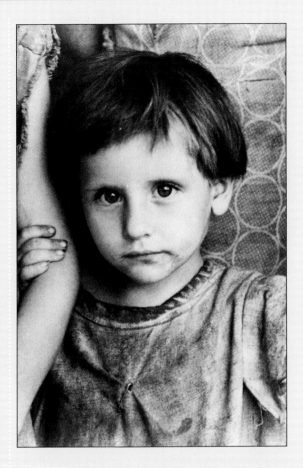

Photograph by Walker Evans of Laura Minnie Lee Tengle, a poor child living with her family in Alabama, 1936.

James Agee worked with photographer Walker Evans on Let Us Now Praise Famous Men.

closely involved with the three families they were reporting on, and Agee depicted them in a personal and novelistic manner, using fiction techniques to portray the individuals, their thoughts, and their feelings. The work was rejected by *Fortune* magazine, which had originally commissioned it, so Agee and Walker instead published it independently. The work, one of the most influential publications of the time in its revelation of the suffering of its subjects, is a remarkable marriage of the historical reliability of nonfiction, the visual accuracy of photography, and the personal detail and interest of fiction.

CHRONICLERS OF THE GREAT DEPRESSION • 113

Walter Lippmann

Newspapers provided a platform for those who wanted to voice their own propaganda. One of the most important progressive thinkers of the 1930s was Walter Lippmann (1889–1974). In his columns and radio broadcasts he advocated a transformation of America's institution. It has been estimated that his opinions reached an average of 10 million Americans every day.

strange things...." The new magazine sold far better than its rivals—one million copies of its first issue—and set a trend that was widely imitated. Photomagazines exploited the public's desire to see what was being described. Their enduring popularity is shown by the fact that many can still be found on magazine racks today.

Protest and Propaganda

The Depression suggested to many American intellectuals that capitalism as a system had failed and that only leftist ideologies would ultimately save America.

Writers such as Mike Gold, Sherwood Anderson (1876–1941), James T. Farrell, Erskine Caldwell, Tillie Olsen, Meridel Le Sueur, and Agnes Smedley all contributed to magazines with Marxist philosophies. They included Mike Gold's own magazine *New Masses*, as well as the *Partisan Review* and *New Republic*.

Such writers did not believe that any political party was capable of solving the country's problems because all parties worked within a system that was fundamentally at fault. Writers criticized the huge discrepancies in wealth in the country and the superficial self-

as Walter Lippmann, whose opinions were syndicated throughout the country (see box).

NEWSMAGAZINES

The hunger for news carried over to magazines. Henry Luce's weekly newsmagazine *Time*, founded in 1923, enjoyed huge growth in the 1930s. By 1933 it faced competition from rivals *Newsweek* and *Today*, which also provided in-depth coverage of the background behind news stories. In response, in 1936 Luce founded *Life*, a more general illustrated newsmagazine. Its declared aim was "To see life; to see the world; to witness great events; to watch the faces of the poor and the gestures of the proud; to see

Front cover of Time *magazine, 1938. The cover illustration, by S. J. Woolf, depicts U.S. aviator Charles Lindbergh (left) and French surgeon Alexis Carrel looking for the fountain of youth.*

TIME

The Weekly Newsmagazine

Painted for TIME by S. J. Woolf

Volume XXXI

LINDBERGH, CARREL & PUMP
They are looking for the fountain of age.
(See MEDICINE)

Number 24

Starr, Kevin. *Endangered Dreams: The Great Depression in California* (Americans and the California Dream). New York: Oxford University Press, 1996.

Ware, Susan. *Holding the Line: American Women in the 1930s.* Boston: Twayne, 1982.

Weiss, Nancy. *Farewell to the Party of Lincoln: Black Politics in the Age of FDR.* Princeton: Princeton University Press, 1983.

CULTURE AND THE ARTS

Benet's Reader's Encyclopedia of American Literature. New York: Harpercollins, 1996.

Davidson, Abraham A. *Early American Modernist Painting, 1910–1935.* New York: Da Capo Press, 1994.

Haskell, Barbara. *The American Century: Art & Culture, 1900–1950.* New York: W. W. Norton & Co., 1999.

Hughes, Robert. *American Visions: The Epic History of Art in America.* New York: Knopf, 1999.

McJimsey, George. *Harry Hopkins: Ally of the Poor and Defender of Democracy.* Cambridge, Mass.: Harvard University Press, 1987.

Meltzer, Milton. *Violins and Shovels: The WPA Arts Projects.* New York: Delacorte Press, 1976.

———. *Dorothea Lange: A Photographer's Life.* Syracuse, NY: Syracuse University Press, 2000.

Pells, R. H. *Radical Visions and American Dreams: Culture and Social Thought in the Depression Years.* Urbana: Illinios University Press, 1998.

Pollack, Howard. *Aaron Copland: The Life and Work of an Uncommon Man.* New York: Henry Holt & Co., Inc., 1999.

Thomson, David. *Rosebud: The Story of Orson Welles.* New York: Vintage Books, 1997.

Wilson, Edmond. *The American Earthquake: A Document of the 1920s and 1930s.* Garden City, NY: Doubleday, 1958.

INTERNATIONAL AFFAIRS

Bullock, Alan. *Hitler: A Study in Tyranny.* New York: Harper and Row, 1962.

Dallek, Robert. *Franklin D. Roosevelt and American Foreign Policy.* New York: Oxford University Press, 1979.

Kindleberger, Charles P. *The World in Depression, 1929–1939.* Berkeley: University of California Press, 1986.

Offner, A. A. *The Origins of the Second World War: American Foreign Policy and World Politics.* Melbourne, FL: Krieger Publishing Company, 1986.

Pauley, B. F. *Hitler, Stalin, and Mussolini: Totalitarianism in the Twentieth Century.* Wheeling, IL: Harlan Davidson, 1997.

Ridley, J. *Mussolini.* New York: St. Martin's Press, 1998.

WEB SITES

African American Odyssey: The Depression, The New Deal, and World War II
http://lcweb2.loc.gov/ammem/aaohtml/exhibit/aopart8.html

America from the Great Depression to World War II: Photographs from the FSA and OWI, 1935–1945
http://memory.loc.gov/ammem/fsowhome.html

The American Experience: Surviving the Dust Bowl
http://www.pbs.org/wgbh/amex/dustbowl

Biographical Directory of the United States Congress
http://bioguide.congress.gov

By the People, For the People: Posters from the WPA, 1936–1943
http://memory.loc.gov/ammem/wpaposters/wpahome.html

Federal Theater Project
http://memory.loc.gov/ammem/fedtp/fthome.html

Huey Long
http://www.lib.lsu.edu/special/long.html

The New Deal Network, Franklin and Eleanor Roosevelt Institute
http://newdeal.feri.org

New York Times Archives
http://www.nytimes.com

Presidents of the United States
http://www.ipl.org/ref/POTUS.html

The Scottsboro Boys
http://www.english.upenn.edu/~afilreis/88/scottsboro.html

Voices from the Dust Bowl: The Charles L. Todd and Robert Sonkin Migrant Worker Collection, 1940–1941
http://memory.loc.gov/ammem/afctshtml/tshome.html

WPA American Life Histories
http://lcweb2.loc.gov/ammem/wpaintro/wpahome.html

PICTURE CREDITS

TIMELINE OF THE DEPRESSION

1929
Hoover creates Farm Board
Stock-market crash (October)

1930
California begins voluntary repatriation of Mexicans and Mexican Americans
Smoot-Hawley Tariff Act
Little Caesar, first great gangster movie of the sound era
Ford cuts workforce by 70 percent (June)
Drought strikes Midwest (September)

1931
Credit Anstalt, Austrian bank, collapses (May 1)
All German banks close (July 13)
Britain abandons gold standard (September 21)

1932
Norris-La Guardia Act
Congress approves Reconstruction Finance Corporation (January 22)
FDR makes "forgotten man" radio broadcast (April 7)
Repression of Bonus Expeditionary Force by Douglas MacArthur (June 17)
Farmers' Holiday Association organizes a farmers' strike (August)
FDR wins a landslide victory in presidential election (November 8)

1933
Fiorello La Guardia elected mayor of New York City.
Nazi leader Adolf Hitler becomes chancellor of Germany
Assassination attempt on FDR by Giuseppe Zangara (February 15)
FDR takes oath as 32nd president of the United States (March 4)
National bank holiday (March 6)
Start of the Hundred Days: Emergency Banking Relief Act (March 9)
FDR delivers first "fireside chat" (March 12)
Economy Act (March 20)
Beer-Wine Revenue Act (March 22)
Civilian Conservation Corps Reforestation Relief Act (March 31)
Emergency Farm Mortgage Act (May)
Federal Emergency Relief Act (FERA) and Agricultural Adjustment Administration (AAA) created (May 12)
Tennessee Valley Authority (May 18)
Federal Securities Act (May 27)
London Economic Conference (June)
Home Owners Refinancing Act (June 13)
Banking Act; Farm Credit Act; Emergency Railroad Transportation Act; National Industrial Recovery Act;

Glass Steagall Banking Act (June 16)
73rd Congress adjourns (June 16)
FDR creates Civil Works Administration (November)

1934
U.S. joins International Labour Organization
Huey Long launches Share-Our-Wealth Society (January)
Farm Mortgage Refinancing Act (January 31)
Securities Exchange Act (June 6)
National Housing Act (June 28)

1935
Emergency Relief Appropriation Act (April 8)
Soil Conservation Act (April 27)
Resettlement Administration created (May 1)
Rural Electrification Administration created (May 11)
Sureme Court rules NIRA unconstitutional (May 27)
Works Progress Administration formed (May 6)
Federal Music Project introduced (July)
National Labor Relations (Wagner) Act (July 5)
Social Security Act (August 14)
Banking Act (August 23)
Public Utility Holding Company Act (August 28)
Farm Mortgage Moratorium Act (August 29)
Revenue Act of 1935 (August 30)
Wealth Tax Act (August 31)
Huey Long dies after assassination (September 10)

1936
FDR wins 1936 election (November 3)
Gone with the Wind published
Charlie Chaplin's *Modern Times* is last great silent movie
Supreme Court rules AAA unconstitutional (January 6)
Soil Conservation and Domestic Allotment Act (1936) (February 29)
Voodoo Macbeth opens in New York (April 14)

1937
Wagner-Steagall National Housing Act (September 1)
Supreme Court axes NLRB
CIO wins a six-week sit-down strike at General Motors plant in Flint, Michigan.
Supreme Court Retirement Act (March 1)
Bituminous Coal Act (April 26)
Neutrality Act of 1937 (May 1)
Farm Tenant Act (July 22)

Revenue Act of 1937 (August 26)
National Housing Act (September 1)
Start of sit-down strike at General Motors Fisher Body Plant in Flint, Michigan, which lasts 44 days (December)

1938
Amended Federal Housing Act (February 4)
Agricultural Adjustment Act (1938) (February 16)
Naval Expansion Act of 1938 (May 17)
Revenue Act of 1938 (May 28)
Food, Drink, and Cosmetic Act (June 24)
Fair Labor Standards Act (June 25)
Orson Welles' *The War of the Worlds* broadcast (October 30)

1939
John Steinbeck's *The Grapes of Wrath* published
Public Works Administration discontinued
Federal Loan Agency created
Supreme Court declares the sit-down strike illegal (February 27)
Administrative Reorganization Act of 1939 (April 3)
Hatch Act (August 2)
Outbreak of World War II in Europe (September 3)
Neutrality Act of 1939 (November 4)

1940
In California the Relief Appropriation Act is passed, raising the period of eligibility for relief from one to three years
Richard Wright's *Native Son* establishes him as the era's leading black author

1941
American Guide series published for the last time
Publication of James Agee and Walker Evans' *Let Us Now Praise Famous Men*
Japanese bomb Pearl Harbor, Hawaii, bringing U.S. into World War II (December 7)

1943
Government eliminates all WPA agencies

1944
Farm Security Administration closed

1945
FDR dies
Japanese surrender

INDEX